AUTOBIOGRAPHY

OF

A REFORMED DRUNKARD;

OR

LETTERS AND RECOLLECTIONS BY AN INMATE OF THE ALMS-HOUSE.

John Cotton Mather

"Madman! Look through my eyes if thou hast none of thine own."

This Book Belongs to:

SA
PIEN
TIA

SCI
EN
TIA

IN
TELLEC
TVS

FOR
TITV
DO

CON
SILI
VM

PI
E
TAS

TIMOR
DÑI

AUTOBIOGRAPHY
OF
A REFORMED DRUNKARD;
OR
LETTERS AND RECOLLECTIONS
BY AN INMATE
OF THE ALMS-HOUSE.

John Cotton Mather

THE TEMPERANCE CRUSADE.
FOUR HOURS IN A BAR ROOM.

1ST HOUR
CYNICAL INDIFFERENCE.

2ND HOUR
MOCKERY AND DEFIANCE.

3RD HOUR
RAGE AND DESPAIR.

4TH HOUR
UNCONDITIONAL SURRENDER.

Table of Contents

New Publisher's Note.. i

Publisher's Foreword.. iii

LETTER No. I... 1

LETTER No. II.. 5

LETTER No. III. 9

LETTER No. IV. 14

LETTER V..19

LETTER VI. 25

LETTER No. VII. 30

LETTER No. VIII. 34

No. I..39

No. II 43

No. III. 49

No. IV. 56

No. V. 61

No. VI. 69

No. VII. 75

No. VIII. 83

No. IX. 89

No. X. 96

Appendix A: 105

DEDICATION
TO
THE WASHINGTONIANS
WHO ARE
SO SUCCESSFULLY FOLLOWING
UP THE LABOURS
OF THE EARLY PIONEERS
IN THE
CAUSE OF TEMPERANCE,
THIS LITTLE WORK IS DEDICATED,
AS A FAITHFUL PORTRAITURE
BOTH OF THE
WOES OF INTEMPERANCE,
AND OF THE
JOYS AND HOPES AND AIMS AND EFFORTS
OF ONE WHO HAS THROUGH MERCY
OBTAINED DELIVERANCE THEREFROM.

A Reformed Drunkard

New Publisher's Note

Blessed beloved bookreader, you have found this volume in your vision. We hope you read on, but let us offer a few humble words. Of making many books there is no end, and a long preface is a chasing after wind. We pray you give us a moment's indulgence.

Our mission is to build a bridge into the past, before film, television, copyright, and internet swallowed up the world. Before 'content' was culture. If the reader finds friends from before the echo chamber, they may find armor and sword against the dreadful noise machine.

We are convinced that many authors and many books are ready to rise like Lazarus and reenter the world to remind the readers that their life has purpose; that their time should be valued; and their history is an honorable home.

This book was chosen because it reveals a forgotten path, a bridge between the modern recovery movement, and the oldest American church tradition. It was written by a storied name, John Cotton Mather, and is an incredible tale of recovery and reformation. The original illustrations, though aged and stained, have been reproduced, because they are illuminating of the author's narrative.

We hope that if your first instinct is to scoff at such a narrative, that you read through and find light in the author's experience, strength and hope.

Your Most Humble and Obedient Servant (YMHOS),

Arthur Bulkington,

Melville Bay

Autobiography Of

Publisher's Foreword

As we conceive it, the duty of a foreword is to make three points.

1) Why we liked it. Why it was worth our time.

2) Why it has relevance today.

3) Why it is worth your precious reading time.

We liked it because it deals with a subject that is one of our hobbyhorses, one of the elements in our mission, an ingredient in our long term plan. We believe, and hope to build on this insight, that there is a divorce between modern 'recovery' and the larger Christian tradition that must be healed and bound back together. This divorce has caused the larger church to give up on many social causes that she should be leading, because the state and the pharmaceutical-insurance industrial complex have monopolized and commoditized the 'recovery movement' and turned it into a 'recovery industry.' This is a larger thesis, for a different time, but this notion has guided our efforts in finding books worth resurrecting from the forgotten archives, and sending out into the world.

We do not want to be pedantic, shrill, or righteous about any of this, but we have arrived at this conclusion through lived experience and wide reading. It is a problem nobody is working on, and it is a problem that will require time and evidence, evidence in the form of a series of books, books that find their readers, in order to plant seeds for future solutions. Future solutions that we hope to build, if our bookmaking venture takes root and begins to bear good fruit.

This is a bit of a tangent. But tangents are the very nature of life, for, as Joyce wrote, "Think you're escaping and run into yourself. Longest way round is the shortest way home."

This is to say that what we found in the book, besides a catchy title, is spiritual paydirt. Whether it sells enough to free us from our dayjobs is besides the point.

This drunkard's autobiography is written by John Cotton Mather, of the Mather family. The Mather family is the non plus ultra of WASPs, a family of ministers stretching back to the 1500s, who played a pivotal role in the founding of Masschussetts and the Puritan settling of New England. They battled witchcraft in Salem. They helped cast out Roger Williams and Anne Hutchinson, who went on to found Rhode Island. They were of the first generation of Harvard students. They are a storied family, the oldest kind of Yankee Bluebloods and Boston Brahmins you could hope to find.

Maybe for this reason, the name of the author is partly obscured with anonymity, and only becomes apparent partway through the narrative. Seeing a leading light of the time take the cloak of anonymity in the 1840s suggests to us that the principle of anonymity is a deep and timeless well, not something new.

We find it to be important that such a goodly family as the Mathers had one of its scions succumb to drunkenness. The horror of that state of mind is recognizable to anyone who has lived it or seen it close up in their loved ones.

In our time, there have been Presidents' Wives and Senators and Secretaries of Health and Human Services who have succumbed to—and recovered from—addiction. It is no respecter of persons, an equal opportunity scourger of souls.

What you will find is a recognizable story of homelessness, wandering, arrests, stupor, shame, and foolishness.

What you will also find are a few colorful scenes, like something out of *Pilgrim's Progress* or the *Divine Comedy*, with allegorical visions of processions of hell, as the demons march triumphantly with enslaved drunkards in train.

And you will find a slice of first person testimony that the Washingtonian Society worked very well for those who fell into its embrace. This is a niche subject known at best to a few AA oldtimers and historians, but finding this book revealed a few more books on them which we hope to bring into the world.

What you will find within is another angle that doesn't map onto the modern recovery movement, which tries to restrain itself from 'outside issues.' That angle is the relentless scorn and anger that the author, John Cotton Mather, poured upon the rum-seller, and the State of Massachussetts. He believes the state manufactures drunkards for profit. He holds the state directly responsible for licensing and profiting from the liquor trade, and does not pull his punches in attacking them or any of the others who profit from his—and other drunkards–misery. The same arguments and attacks he makes upon the liquor trade could be readily applied to the many 'legal' drugmakers and the many doctors who prescribe them.

It might have made sense for the early AA movement to sidestep the decades-long issues of 'wet' and 'dry' and Prohibition, in order to survive and focus on helping others. That is no longer the case, and now there is noone with any power or willingness to push back against the many institutions and people who profit off of the misery of millions who are suffering from chemical dependency. Neither the Church nor any recovery group says anything about these issues.

All that is to say, we see his story, and his anger, as a deeply relevant corrective and antidote to the shortcomings of the modern Church, which lives tax-free and spends its energies on either endlessly litigating social war issues it does not have the authority to solve, on mission trips abroad, and on chiding men to 'man up;' and the modern recovery movement enmeshed as it is in psychobabble, prescription drugs, Hollywood sensibilities, "harm reduction," and New Age fads. All while the recovery rate plummets and overdose deaths continue to reach new record numbers.

This is a pretty solid answer to points 1 and 2, why we liked it, and why it's relevant. We will let you infer the rest, and we may write about this topic ourselves in the future.

Why would this be relevant to you, Dear Reader?

We expect our first audience will be a certain slice of twitter users, who are predominantly cosmopolitan, yet call themselves conservative or 'right wing.' Sensitive Young Men alienated from their consumerist peers and disempowered by decades of policy choices. Perhaps they have found themselves abusing substances, and perhaps this narrative suggests a way out.

Yet it's possible this group likely has little interest in such a narrative. Either because it has never had to deal with these issues, or because this issue cannot be quickly and simply weaponized to score political points online. But we should note that the drug war industry, the cartels, the pharmaceutical industry, the insurance industry, all have a vested interest in 'business as usual,' and will not be stopped by internet posting, and will not be stopped by money. It will take a great movement and great power to change things.

But we also hope to reach the more obvious audiences, like Christians, like people in recovery. It is for those people that this book was resurrected. We believe that the path between recovery meetings and churches has been blocked, by disuse, by design, by lack of knowledge, and we believe this book can help retrace a trail between those two points, and strengthen both.

We sincerely hope that this foreword has piqued your interest. We believe if you have found this book, it is meant for you.

Your Most Humble and Obedient Servant (YMHOS),

Arthur Bulkington,

Melville Bay

A Reformed Drunkard

ADVERTISEMENT.

THE "Letters from the Alms-house" were first published in a popular periodical. The "Recollections" are simply a continuation of the narrative begun in the "Letters."

The desire has been often expressed, in various quarters, especially by the friends of the Temperance Reformation, that these articles should be put into a more permanent shape, for general circulation; and it is in compliance with these requests that this edition of them is issued.

A miserably printed and spurious edition of the "Letters," without the "Recollections," was published some time since without the knowledge of the author.

February, 1845.

LETTER No. I

LAST week I was put into this place, and how and wherefore I will tell you. It was my last debauch, which the liberty of this free country (so freely enjoyed by the drunkards of Norwich) permitted me to go through, even to lying in the gutter, the height, or rather depth of liberty. There as I lay in my drunken dream, methought the American eagle was perched just over against me, holding in his bill a chart, having thereon golden letters. The largest of them read thus—*A LICENSE TO MAKE DRUNKARDS*,—and underneath was the license law. I thought the eagle looked rather muddy in the eye, and flapped his wings as lazily and awkwardly as drunken men manage their legs. In my ears all the while rung the words, *drunk by authority of the State of Connecticut.* Where the voice came from I could not see, but there it was, and repeated without cessation, *drunk by authority of the State of Connecticut.* Humph! humph! said I, rather a queer authority. The voice had just at this moment uttered the word *drunk*, but it added in a low note, with a suppressed laugh, I think so too, and then went on to finish the sentence with its wonted gruff tone, *by authority of the State of Connecticut.*

It seemed a familiar voice to my ear, and at length I thought it sounded very much like the voice of a friend of mine, a rum-selling Justice of the Peace, who manufactures the article called drunkard, and then sends it away to its proper storehouse, the alms-house, charging cartage, &c., to the town. "What I" thought I, "are you drunk too, you that sit on the seat of judgment, 'a terror to evil-doers, and a praise to them that do well? And why not? for it is just as proper for you to get drunk yourself as to make others so 'by authority of the State of Connecticut' and more proper, if anything; for then it is a concern of your own, and if you only go to bed and sleep it out, (as I presume you do,) you avoid disturbing that peace of which you are the Justice." Whether it was his voice I could not tell; but it kept on and on, *drunk by authority of the State of Connecticut*, till I was tired of its dull monotony, and was glad to be waked by "the authority of the State of Connecticut" in another shape, and with another voice. I thought the old eagle had got so drunk as to tumble over upon me, and was flapping his wings about my ears but as I waked, I found it was a constable pulling me by the shoulders by the "authority of the State of Connecticut," for this, it seems, was the presiding genius of the scene throughout. "Here, sir—here, sir, get up," said he.

"Who gave you authority to disturb me?" "The State of Connecticut, you scoundrel." "Well, sir," said I, "I got drunk by the 'authority of the State of Connecticut,' and I think I have a right to sleep it out by that same authority." "You've got to go to the workhouse, and—" "O well," said I, " I'll go, for it's very well that after getting drunk by 'authority of the State of Connecticut,' the State should give me a shelter— there's consistency in it, and that's a jewel. I'll go, I'll go." And he hurried me away. He brought me to the office of a Justice of the Peace, where was straightway assembled a motley group, rubicund and pale-faced, well-dressed and ill-dressed, drunk and sober, all with eyes, ears, and mouth wide open. I confessed my crime, that is that I had been drunk several days, and that too by 'authority of the State of Connecticut.'

"I took care," said I, "to proceed legally in the matter, this being a country of *law* as well as *liberty*, and bought nearly all that I drank of those who were *legally* authorized to sell. I can name them, if it please your honour." "That is not essential," said, the Justice quickly, with a shrug of his shoulders, and the people looked into each other's faces and laughed. "I admire your laws,"[1] continued I, "for if a poor fellow gets into trouble as I have, by obeying the laws so scrupulously as to get drunk *legally*, he is put into a snug place where he can get sober and comfortable again. I shall go cheerfully to your alms-house. How long, sir, must I be kept there." "As you have been seen drunk at two different times, I shall sentence you there for sixty days." "That's too long," said I; "does your law punish a man twice for the same offence ?" "Certainly not." "Well, then, your sentence is not legal. I have been drunk without cessation for a whole week, it's all one offence, and you can't make two of it." "Sixty days

---

1   Anatole France, 'The law, in its majestic equality, forbids rich and poor alike to sleep under bridges, to beg in the streets, and to steal their bread.'

is the sentence," said he in a firm voice; and Justices have a way of cutting things short which we poor fellows must submit to, even though we get drunk strictly in the form and manner prescribed by the authority of the State of Connecticut.

As the constable and I went to the almshouse, we had some little chat together. I heard some one call him Mr. Green, and happened to recollect that when I was once before in this place, I bought some rum of him. "You are a rum-seller, I believe, are you not, sir ?" said I. "No sir." "Well you once was." "Y—es," said he, rather reluctantly. "So you have left off making people drunk by 'authority of the State of Connecticut,' and have gone into another branch of the business under that 'authority'—taking care of the poor fellows after they are drunk[2]—I suppose you might attend to both branches at once, as I believe is sometimes done, and then you would never be in want of subjects to get constable's fees out of." He was not much disposed to talk with me, and when he delivered me over to the keeper he said, "you've got an odd fellow this time."

Here I am, in an alms-house—I who was formed to enjoy life and to adorn it—I who have friends of high standing in society, that have borne with me until endurance ceased to be a virtue—I who have the blood of the Puritans in my veins—who have sprung from a noble and ancient family, a family that has supplied the pulpit, the bar, and the senate with many of their best ornaments— yes, I even I, am in an alms-house. From a giddy height have I fallen to this abyss of degradation. Though I do not wish to make out my guilt to be any less than it really is, I verily believe that I never should have been a drunkard if the *customs* and *laws* of society were such as they should be. These have offered temptations strong on every hand, and have made futile every attempt at reformation. The customs of society, it is true, have been much improved by the temperance efforts of the past twelve years, but the laws in this State yet continue to be utterly at variance with justice and the public good. The "authority of the State of Connecticut" is certainly used

2   In 2025, the 'recovery industry' is about $80-100 billion a year. And overdose deaths continue to rise, and recovery rates shrink. Many people are funneled into this industry from the criminal justice system.

for some very bad purposes.

I have been here long enough to recover both in body and mind from my debauch. Reason is again on the throne, and I hope it is something more than one of those *lucid intervals*[3] of which I have had so many before. At any rate, so much do I in these sober moments abhor intemperance, and all the influences that lead men into it, that I am ready to do any thing to save others from the bitter woes that I have suffered. And as the good keeper is willing to supply me with pen, ink, and paper, I propose to give you a sort of *portraiture* of intemperance, during the few weeks that I stay here. I know it all in its darkest and most hideous shades, and I shall paint it all, let who will be offended. My motto will be, "nothing extenuate, nor set down aught in malice." The evil customs, and the more evil laws, I shall not spare, but shall hurl at them, with the little strength that intemperance has left me, the shafts both of reason and ridicule.

Yours, &c.

---

3   Big Book, pg. 90 "Don't deal with him when he is very drunk, unless he is ugly and the family needs your help. Wait for the end of the spree, or at least for a lucid interval."

LETTER No. II.

My DEAR FRIEND,

IN this epistle I shall relate some of the incidents that transpired during the few days that I spent in the rum-holes of this place. Though I do not remember to have seen Rum, or Gin, or Brandy on any sign in your town, the forty drunkard-making shops have an abundance of these articles, as I know, for I have seen them sell them freely. As I entered the place, just intoxicated enough to be limber-tongued, I met a man in a similar condition, and having a fellow-feeling we soon got well acquainted. I asked him where I could get some rum. "O, almost any where," said he. "There's a shop (pointing across the way) kept by Mr. James, one of the best men that ever was." "But how do you know that he sells it? There's no sign out with rum on it; there's *Molasses, Beef, Pork, Meal, Candles*, but no *Rum*." Says he, "don't you see Ale there? That means such things now-a-days. These cold-water folks have made such a rumpus, they don't put *Rum, Gin, Brandy*, and so on, up and down their shutters as they used to. So, friend, when you find *Ale* outside, you can generally find *Rum* inside, and perhaps no Ale. Why, the best row I ever had was in a shop with 'New York Porter House' on the sign—there was every thing there but porter. There's another thing, too; if you ever see oysters, or confectionery, or refreshments on a shop, there's a pretty good chance of finding the ardent there." "A little ashamed of their business after all. Does Mr. James sell under the authority of the State of Connecticut?" "O yes; he's got a license. Its a legal business. Our legislature and civil authority have no priestcraft. They believe in a man's taking a little once in a while." "And some of them love it themselves," said I, "and some of them so love the dear people that love it, that they are careful not to meddle with the divine right of getting drunk, or the divine right of making others drunk." "You are a curious fellow—sort of drunken cold-water man, I guess." "I guess I am," said I, and went into the shop. Every thing looked very decent, and I couldn't see any thing like a rum cask. I saw, however, a man drinking in the back part of the shop, and as he went out he put some money on the counter without saying a word. I asked Mr. James if he sold rum.

He stared at me a moment, and then coming up to me asked me in a very low tone, how much I wanted. He seemed very much afraid that he should be heard by some men that stood by the door, (some of his cold-water customers, I presume.) After he had filled my bottle, I asked him why he had no sign out with Rum on it. He hesitated a moment, and then said, "it is not the fashion, sir." "People that are patronised by kings or queens," said I, "are very careful to make it known, and I think the authority of the State of Connecticut is enough of a queen to be proud of her favour. I recommend to you to put up on your door, and get stamped on all your jugs and bottles something like this— *Drunkard-maker to the State of Connecticut; or, to the Honourable the Senate and House of Representatives*" I saw that the gentlemen that stood about the door were listening, and were coming in one after another, so I went on. "I wonder if your rum is pure. Some, you know, water it, and then pepper it with something to make it taste strong enough. But what you sell must be good, as you are an authorized agent of the State. However, I'll try it," putting the bottle to my mouth—"O, I forgot that the law forbids you to let people drink on your premises. Well, I can go out of doors and drink, though I don't exactly see the difference between getting drunk inside of your shop and outside of it, so long as you supply the rum. But laws are sometimes very nice in their distinctions, and there may be a reason for this one that a lawyer may see, though I cannot" One of the gentlemen advised me to throw away my bottle, and be a sober man. "Good advice," said I, "but I can't do it. I have an appetite that I cannot resist; I feel its burnings within me now, and I can't help being drunk,[4] as long as these faithful agents of the public will sell rum. They all know—Mr. James knows—that drunkards have this appetite, and they minister to it for filthy lucre's sake. I know how it will be with me from what has been. I shall go on for a week or ten days, till my bodily energies are so exhausted that I can go no farther, and then I shall get sober again. You," pointing to Mr. James, "agent for the public in this matter, are helping me in this course. I am a drunkard, you

---

4   Big Book, pg. xxix, "These men were not drinking to escape; they were drinking to overcome a craving beyond their mental control."

are a drunkard-maker. I, urged on by appetite, am the victim of your avarice. If there ever was a dirty way of making money, it is this. You wonder, gentlemen, that a drunkard will talk thus; but I tell you that I hate both the fetters that bind me, and the men that forge them." "That's plain talk," said the retailer, who looked as if he would be glad to have me gone. "Well I mean to be plain. I wish you would be as plain with your conscience; you would empty every rum cask into the street, and curse the day you went into this business." "It's pretty well for a dirty, ragged drunkard to lecture me in this way." "Your business is to make just such dirty, ragged drunkards as I am—so don't find fault with your own work." "A fair hit," said one of the company.

As I went out of the shop, I saw some Mohegan Indians[5] at a little distance, emptying a jug which they got filled at this same decent shop of the decent Mr. James—another beautiful example of the consistency of the laws of our wise Daniels. The law opens here and there a fountain of drunkenness, appoints a keeper to deal out its precious contents, but orders him to permit no one to drink just around the fountain, though any one can drink as much, and get as drunk as he pleases, if he is only outside of the walls that enclose it. The apothecary would be just as reasonable if he should tell a man that wanted to kill himself with poison, I'll sell it to you, on condition that you shall get out of the shop before you take it. What matters it to the wife and children of the drunkard that are beaten and turned out of doors, whether he got drunk on the spot where he bought the rum, or by the way, or after he had reached home? According to my notion, (and I ought to know something about it, for I have been drunk in many different spots in my life,) getting drunk is the same thing in all places, whether it be outside of a shop or inside—in a licensed shop or in an unlicensed one. Getting drunk is getting drunk; and such a wise legislature as your Connecticut legislature is, cannot make any thing else of it. The only difference that I can see is this—that a man who gets drunk in a shop may walk some of the steam off, and may not be as drunk

---

5   The Mohegan Nation still exists on a reservation in Connecticut. They signed a treaty of friendship with the Puritans in 1630. The alcohol trade was especially hard on Native Americans.

when he gets home, as he would be if he waited till then, so that, on the whole, it is better to get drunk in the shop than at home; and I would recommend to our legislators to consider this fact, and lay a penalty on making people drunk outside of the shop instead of inside, as the law now stands.

And I would recommend farther, for the good of drunkards' families, that every keeper of a fountain of drunkenness should be obliged to take care of every man he makes drunk, till he gets sober. This would certainly be just, for the keeper is the only one profited by making him drunk. Suppose the law were so—what a pretty scene would a rum-shop present at night when some twenty or thirty were drunk—some staggering about, some vomiting, some dead drunk, some singing with an occasional hiccup by way of symphony or trill, and some with slippery tongues, cursing priestcraft and the cola-water society. And what a scene, too, next morning, when the door is opened, and the light of the sun, which shines alike upon the just and the unjust, is let in upon them. Bah! the very thought nauseates me, and I cannot describe it—it's beyond description.

Here I must stop, and I will give you the rest of the incidents of the week in my next.

Yours, &c.

LETTER No. III.

DEAR SIR,

ONE morning I saw a country retailer going out of town with a loaded wagon, and as he seemed to be in some trouble, I went up to him and offered my assistance. I found that a rum cask had sprung a leak. A good many gathered around, and a variety of remarks were made. "It would be well if all the rum were poured out," said one. "What a stench," said another. "It smells good," said a ragged, pale-faced fellow, with an oath, to his red-faced neighbour. "Pouring your rum into the street, eh? I'm glad to see it, Mr. Gridley," said a gentleman passing by. This occasioned a titter among the bystanders, and Mr. Gridley looked rather ashamed. I could point out every man there that was a drunkard, from the expression of his countenance; there was a longing look fastened on the muddy liquor not to be mistaken.

After leaving this scene, I went into a rum hole where I found two sailors, that I got acquainted with in New London. Here we charged high, and then we took a ride in a wagon together. They had driven the horse so outrageously that he was rather reluctant to go—but we soon got him well under way. We drove full tilt against a country wagon, with two buxom damsels in it, that had come in to do their Saturday shopping. And here I would say, that if your public authorities authorize men to make drunkards, they ought to make the streets wide enough for drunkards to drive in. Well, the ladies were near being turned out, but experienced no other damage than the crushing of a band-box containing a go to-meeting bonnet. But *we* struck against a post and were capsized upon the pavement. We were so drunk that we were not hurt by the fall. I apologized to the ladies for demolishing the bonnet, and told them that I had no funds, but would give them an order on the man that made us drunk, if that would do. I thought it was fair that he should endorse our driving. I expected that the constable and justice would make a good job out of our case, for the fees they would get for putting three of us in the work-house, would make a sum not to be despised. But for some reason or other no notice was taken of the affair.

Rum-sellers often make a great *show* of being scrupulous about the individuals to whom they sell. I met a fellow the other day coming out of a shop swearing roundly because the keeper of it would let him haye no rum. He was not very drunk—not enough to stagger, at least on even ground, and the shop I knew, by former experience, to be not the most decent that could be found, so that I wondered a little at the refusal. The riddle, however, was soon solved. I found there were some very respectable looking men in the shop, and this produced all at once a scrupulous fit in the rum seller. After they went away, there came in a red-faced fellow, much more drunk than he that was sent away empty; but the *scruple* was gone and the *dram* was sold him. "Well Natty, was that good rum ?" "Yes, yes," said he, smacking his lips ; "I like something that I can hear from, and I'll swear there's no water in that. There's no mistake in rum and sugar,"—and he staggered out of the shop. As I sat there I saw many come in to take their dram, and among them was a boy of fifteen, smoking his segar and swearing, and a lame old man of nearly eighty, and last of all came in the man who was so unceremoniously refused a little while before. He understood the matter; he knew that he would not be refused now that the cold-water men were gone.

Rum, like wine, (I repeat it—*like wine*,) makes men very wise, very eloquent, very brave, and very loving—that is, unless they get *too* drunk. I saw, the other day, examples of all these effects within a stone's throw of each other. I heard one man asserting that he could prove any thing in law, theology, or medicine. A little way on, I saw a fellow with animated gesture, talking to a knot of idlers about priestcraft and the liberties of the people. Just then another, as he staggered along, said to his companion, "I'm not afraid of him, nor the constable, nor the—the devil," raising his voice to a pretty loud pitch at the climax; and then (*O Cupid, how Bacchus and the modern god of rum do serve thy cause!*) I saw an Irishman, just as he went aboard your steamboat, put his arms around a damsel and squeeze her most lustily, giving her a good smack, and as the boat went off, he stood in her stern waving his hat.

Drunkards are apt to be early risers. The gnawing within, after being so long without rum, wakes them and sends them forth to seek relief. As I came along one morning to Mr. Brinker's shop, I found half-a-dozen or more waiting for him to come and cool their burnings. Such a sorry-looking set I never saw before. There they stood with their hands in their pockets, shivering and spitting, occasionally turning their eye, with a most woeful look in the direction in which he was to come. And as they saw him turn the corner there was almost a shout; they were a new set of men at once. One of the poor fellows, after taking his dram, fell down in a fit. The rum-seller and his company concluded that it was not caused by the rum that he drank there, because he had not had it down long enough. "Then," said I, "Mr. Brinker, you do think rum sometimes produces fits." "Y—es, sometimes," said he. "If a man takes too much," added a fellow half-seas over, "but I don't believe it hurts any body to drink moderately." "Nor I," echoed the whole company. One of them said, "he's subject to fits; it isn't drinking." This seemed to be a great relief to Mr. Brinker; but it was a still greater relief to him to have the poor fellow carried home. Rum sellers dislike to have the results of their horrid traffic stare them in the face.

I have as yet described no night scenes in the rum-shops. They are often perfectly horrid. One night I became so drunk that the keeper of the shop was obliged to provide for me for the night. After having a good long nap, I awoke; and as no one seemed to be aware that I was awake, I lay there looking upon their midnight orgies. It was a Saturday night, and therefore they were more prolonged than usual. The shutters were closed, so that no light was to be seen by the passers by. The besotted faces of the drunkards, as they sat round the gambling table, made a frightful scene as the lights shone dimly on them. But gambling was not the worst thing done in this "suburb of hell." Two females were brought in by the keeper at midnight. Startle not, gentle reader, such abominations do verily exist in this community. I heard this same grog-shop keeper the other day, "agreeing exactly" with a very respectable rum-seller, who said he was willing to join people in putting down intemperance, but that things were carried too far. O these *respectable* rum-sellers! they are a shield for the vilest pests of society. In truth they have a common interest with them in opposing temperance; for their "craft" is the same, and it is in danger to be set at naught. And if it would not endanger this respectability, they would join the dirty dram sellers and ragged drunkards in the cry, Down with the cold-water men.

The next day (Sunday) I passed in this den of iniquity. Many, very many came there, entering by a back door, the front of the shop being perfectly closed. Among them was a Mr. Dilworth, a half-crazed, short, dapper, little man, who was constantly replying to every remark that he liked, "that's grammatically spoken." Old Dilly, as he was called, was a real grog-shop oracle. There was another fellow, whom they called Capt. Pepper, with a big red nose and sore eyes, (caused as he said by a 'sipelas humour,) that was one of the great talkers of the company. There was a Mr. Smith, of about twenty, who, though so young, seemed to be an important character among the loafers; he was a very knowing man, and had a deal to say about priestcraft, aristocrats, &c. The rest of the company had nothing about them particularly observable, but exhibited the common characteristics of drunkards, a smutty face and ragged clothes. There came in a Mr. Ramsey, with a shoe on one foot and a boot on the other, and other things to compare, and he seemed to be quite welcome. He told them, however, that he could not stay long, for his wife was sick. "What's the matter with her," said Captain Pepper. "She's got a fever," said he, " and I thought some spirit would be good to put on outside, and so I've come after it." The Captain then told a long story about his wife once having a fever, and the doctors giving her over, and asserted that she was cured at last by putting a cloth wet in rum on her bowels. He concluded by saying, I really believe rum is a good thing in fevers,"—to which old Dilly replied, "that's grammatically spoken." Though Mr. Ramsay seemed to believe all this, he staid by and put the rum into his own stomach, instead of applying it to his wife's skin. In fact he did not reach home until evening, and his wife died that night—probably the rum was not applied soon enough to save her. Captain Pepper said *his* wife was almost sick. "The old woman is very weakly," said he; "but since these cold-water times have come on, I can't get her to drink anything stimulating. This morning she almost fainted away fixing off the children for Sunday-school." "Sunday-school!" said Mr. Smith, with the most ineffable contempt, and he went on with a tremendous tirade against every thing that was good, all which the company applauded, and old Dilly pronounced to be "grammatically spoken." The conversation at length was turned upon temperance. Mr. Smith very gravely declared that he thought they carried things too far, and that 'Squire Lawson was right when he said that some people were very intemperate in their temperance. "That's grammatically spoken," said old Dilly. "That Squire Lawson is a liberal-minded fellow," said Captain Pepper, "we must have him up for the Gineral 'Sembly next year."

The conversation was very much of this sort through the whole day. But I have given you enough to show you what a grog-shop is on Sunday.

Old Dilly and Captain Pepper are now with me in the Alms-House, and they may be introduced to the notice of your readers again.

We have had the past week a horrible case of delirium tremens in the house. The poor fellow chased dogs, cats, rats, and devils incessantly for several days and nights: and just before he died he thought he was in hell, and the devils were all around him, with all, sorts of instruments of torture. "I'm in hell, in hell!" he would cry. "O! O! don't burn me so!—how that devil bites!" Such perfect terror I never witnessed.[6] The night that he died I had a dreadful dream which I will relate in my next.

Yours, &c.

---

6   Big Book pg. 151, "Some of us sought out sordid places, hoping to find understanding companionship and approval. Momentarily we did—then would come oblivion and the awful awakening to face the hideous Four Horsemen—Terror, Bewilderment, Frustration, Despair. Unhappy drinkers who read this page will understand!"

LETTER No. IV.

DEAR SIR,

THE dream which I had the night that the man died of delirium tremens, I will now relate:—

I dreamed that I witnessed the TRIUMPHAL PROCESSION OF ALCOHOL. The god of Alcohol[7] reposed upon a car *before* which came in long procession those who aid him in his conquests, and *behind* it were arranged, as was the custom in the triumphal processions of ancient heroes, the numerous trophies of his victories. I will describe it in the same order that it passed before me.

The whole was under the guidance of a large number of rather satanic looking charracters, who acted as marshals on the occasion. The time was midnight, and thick darkness covered the earth. Torches were carried by the devils, which sent forth a yellow flame with a tinge of blue. This gave a strange and appalling appearance to every object, and of course made the horrid objects that I saw still more horrid. From the fumes which loaded the air, I supposed the burning materials to be spirit and brimstone.

First in the procession came a very grave looking body of men dressed in black. These were clergymen of various denominations, with a multitude of deacons, elders, churchwardens, &c. In front of them marched a very solemn personage, holding aloft a book on which I saw inscribed in large letters,

PASSAGES OF SCRIPTURE,

INTERPRETED

By that most learned and acute of all Commentators,

DIABOLUS.

Next came legislators, justices of the peace, &c., headed by a man having a banner with this motto—*Every lawful business must be*

7   Big Book, pg. 151, "As we became subjects of King Alcohol, shivering denizens of his mad realm, the chilling vapor that is loneliness settled down."

legally protected. Then followed a motley set, whom I discovered by the mottos on their banners, to be moderate drinkers. Their mottos were—*The good creature of God—A little is good—Down with ultraism—Moderation in all things—Temperance, not total abstinence.*— Next to these came a multitude who seemed to be the very pink of respectability—wholesale dealers, distillers, and men who let their shops for the traffic. The inscriptions on their banners were on this wise—*A respectable and legal business—We are not responsible for the abuse of Ardent Spirit, &c. &c.* Directly behind them came a low-lived, mean-looking crew. They were the dram-sellers. They were preceded by a man bearing on the top of a stick an enormous rum glass, with strings of cents jingling about it. I read on their banners—*Liberty and equality—We, the people—Down with priest-craft—Down with Church and State—We must live.* Some of their banners were the same with those which were carried by the moderate drinkers.

This scurvy crew, the dram-sellers, were throwing their dirty caps into the air, and crying out, *Great is the God of Alcohol.* The very decent and respectable gentlemen before them looked back occasionally with great complacency, and some of them once in a while *faintly* joined in the shout, the fear of tarnishing their *respectability* forbidding a full echo of the shouting of their filthy friends, the dram-sellers.

Next came the car on which reposed the god, which I will attempt to describe. It was not drawn, but was self-moving, the power being in the wheels. These were four hogsheads of Rum, Brandy, Wine, and Whiskey, and they made a dreadful rumbling as they went. The body of the car was figured all over with drinking scenes, from the champaigne party down to the worst scenes of the vilest dram-shop. The projecting front of the car was surmounted with a figure holding a cup to its mouth, with a silly leer on its face. There was a canopy above, and on its cornice were represented bottles, labelled as you see them on a bar-room shelf, Brandy, Gin, Old Spirit, Rum, Madeira, Sherry, &c. From the mouths of the bottles issued the same kind of flame as that of the torches. Alternated with these were faces of all the varied expressions and appearances that drunkenness presents. The self-complacent look; the silly laugh; the besotted face of the old drunkard, with its grisly locks; the doltish face of a man dead drunk, and so on. On the top of the canopy was an animal evidently of swinish origin. Behind the car was fastened a box, on which was inscribed *Pandoras Box*. What a car! how befitting the God that drunkards worship. How many are crushed under the wheels of this American Juggernaut![8] The satanic marshals were constantly busy in bringing victims to throw down before it, and the goa seemed to be delighted with the motion which the crushing of these poor creatures gave to his car. There were unearthly figures dancing about the car, with all sorts of instruments, but there was no harmony; it was a din of discord. A few of them continually repeated in a sort of recitative, these words—*War, famine, pestilence slay their thousands, but Alcohol slays its thousand thousands*. And the instruments would strike up a chorus of horrid discords, such as one would suppose could be made only in hell itself.

Behind the car followed all the multifarious *trophies* of Alcohol. First came a multitude of drunkards, staggering, dancing, fighting, and performing all sorts of antics. The hell like chorus of the instruments about the car seemed to keep them in constant motion, and they echoed it with a drunkard's shout Their appearance was exceedingly grotesque. They were pale-faced, and red-faced, and occasionally a bottle-nose—some with torn, slouched hats, some covered with rags, some lame and limping, some with a boot on one foot and a shoe on the other, and some barefooted; and all had the mark of the beast in some way or other upon them. I perceived constant accessions to their numbers. These were brought by the satanic marshals from the ranks of the moderate drinkers ahead, where they had put themselves without a right so to do. Directly behind these was a car especially devoted to those who were dead drunk. O what a mass of disgusting brutality! The top of this car was graced with a swinish animal of monstrous dimensions.

Next came the inmates of the Alms-House, young and old,

---

8   12&12, p. 37 "Each of us has had his own near-fatal encounter with the juggernaut of self-will, and has suffered enough under its weight to be willing to look for something better."

decrepit and lame, some straight and some bent over, some sore-eyed, some crazy, and some showing the marks of puling idiocy. Among them walked pale-faced, weeping women, carrying and leading half-naked, squalid children, while their husbands walked behind them, with hands in pocket and shrugged shoulders, a per-fect per-sonification of laziness. Then followed a car containing the sick of all sorts. Among others I noticed particularly a thin, gaunt fellow, coughing with all his might—another man lying down, with turgid, purple face, as if in apoplexy—another with every muscle in spasmodic action—another swelled to bursting with dropsy—and another, a woman, with disheveled hair, in convulsions. The body of this car was lettered all over with such words as these—*Consumption, Dropsy, Apoplexy, Convulsions, Fever, &c. &c.* After this came some representations of scenes which could not be acted out. There was a drunken row with its torn clothes, bunged eyes, and flying clubs and brickbats. There was a man drawing his wife along by the hair. There was another with a club, driving a woman and children out of doors. There were a man and woman fighting with shovel and tongs. There was a man with an axe running after a woman, and another cutting his wife's throat with a carving knife. These and other similar scenes were represented in transparencies, and made a very prominent part of the display of the occasion.

After these followed criminals of all sorts, and such a horrid set of faces I never saw. There were vice and passion of every kind de-picted boldly in the countenance. Some of them carried their clank-ing chains. There was the murderer with all his ferocity, the adulter-er with wanton look, the cunning thief, the bold, highway robber, the accomplished counterfeiter, the young harlot with painted face, and the old harlot with dingy blanched skin, and hollow rancorous voice, the most disgusting object of earth.

Last of all came a corps of devils, chanting in recitative these words—*Great are thine earthly trophies, O God of Alcohol; but the wonders of thy might are fully shown only in the hell from whence we came.*

Here my dream ended. I awoke trembling like an aspen leaf,

and the sweat stood in great drops upon me. I hope I shall not be indicted for dreaming, as Deacon Giles' Mr. Cheever was.[9] But I would say that if any one who is implicated in any way in the traffic in ardent spirit, thinks he is meant in any part of the dream, he is right. He no doubt had his place in that triumphal procession of his god Alcohol.

Yours, &c.

---

9   We have included these two stories in the appendix.

LETTER V.

DEAR SIR,

MR. Babcock the keeper of the Alms-House, says that every body is asking him who this dreamer is. Gentle reader, be patient, and I will tell you by and by, and give you my history in full. But I must first give you some account of a few of my associates in the Almshouse. They have made a sort of Father Confessor of me, and the histories of some of them so well illustrate the influence of the causes of intemperance that I will relate them.

I will first introduce you into a room occupied by four women, that meek looking woman that sits in the corner, reading her bible, is Mrs. Rawley. She might once have been handsome, but her troubles have left such slight vestiges of her beauty that they are discoverable only when lighted up by a smile, and then scarcely so except to one who recollected her in her youthful days. She is one of a numerous class of society that have been the prey of care and anxiety and fear for many and many a year, whose dream of happiness in their honey moon, lasted scarcely longer than that short period, and then proved really a dream—all since that having been darkness and woe, except once in a while a little season of sunshine through the opening clouds which served only to make the darkness still more appalling. Oh! to be the victim of the capricious cruelty of a drunkard day after day, week after week, month after month, and year after year! How does woman, lovely, patient woman, bear this worst of earthly woes almost without repining; returning kindness and not reproaches for cruelty, and clinging to the inflicter of it, because the husband of her bosom, and the father of her children, till the last gleam of hope in his case is gone.[10] This is a slow martyrdom, in which Christianity displays some of her noblest virtues. And it very often has its rewards even in this life. The children reared under the influence of mothers tried in this hottest furnace of affliction, very

---

10   Big Book, pg.104, "But for every man who drinks others are involved—the wife who trembles in fear of the next debauch; the mother and father who see their son wasting away."

often become, in spite of the wicked example of the father, bright ornaments of society, and thus bind up the broken hearts of their mothers.

Mrs. Rawley had known no such comforts; her's had been an *unbroken* course of sorrow. She had borne ten children, and is now enciente. She has lost all her children except three, and one of these, the little boy that you see playing with a string by her side, is almost an idiot. Amidst all the sickness and death that have invaded her household, she has had no affectionate husband to cheer her by his sympathies, but instead, a fault-finding, cursing, cruel monster to abuse her.

"The birth of our first child," said she, "was a happy event. All since that have been born in sorrow. It was not till some months after this event that I became convinced of my husband's intemperate habits. O that dreadful night I never shall forget it. Our little one was sick, and I was watching over it with all that solicitude which a mother feels for her first-born. I wondered why my husband was so late. At length he staggered in, and I could hardly have been more shocked, if he had been brought in dead. I had indeed seen something before that excited momentary suspicion. He was sometimes cross, and did not speak to me as he was wont to do. But my affection for him prompted me to find an excuse for all this in the perplexities of his business. Those who have been similarly situated with me will not wonder that it needed the evidence of actual intoxication to convince me of the fact. I did not upbraid him—I could not,—I could only shed bitter tears all the live-long night over my sick child, while he slept like a brute;—and they were bitter tears, more bitter than any I have shed since, except at his death. That *first* revelation of my wretchedness overpowered me; since that I have been so used to weeping that I scarcely find any bitterness in tears. From this time matters grew worse and worse. There were some occasional reformations, but they were very temporary. Though he would weep over his sins and profess repentance and a determination to do better, temptation easily overcame him; and temptation, you know, is every where in the path of the laboring man. Once as he recovered from a long fit of sickness, I really felt very much encouraged about him. He even went so far as to give me permission to go and tell every man that had ever sold him rum to sell him no more. I went forth with some confidence, but I returned broken-hearted. Some few of them seemed to have some proper feeling, but most taunted me with cold-blooded cruelty. One said, "I never sold to your husband when he was not sober." Another said, "This is a land of liberty. If he wants rum he can buy it, and its none of my business what he does with it." Another said, "If I don't sell to him others will." Another, a licensed retailer, said, "I never sell to him to drink in my shop"—just as if it made any difference to me whether he drank the rum there or somewhere else; and besides he knew that he was telling a downright falsehood. At one shop the keeper and his customers laughed me in the face, and one of them said, "You'll never make old Rawley a cold water-man," at which they all gave a shout.

"It was but a short time after his recovery that he came home intoxicated. He obtained his liquor of the licensed retailer whom I just mentioned. *O! the tender mercies of a rum seller*! For the paltry profit of a few cents, he was willing to incur the responsibility of renewing all my misery.

"My husband now became desperate. He was ill-natured not merely when drunk, but at all times; he had a hell in his bosom, and its heavings were always visible. His recollection of his vain attempt at reformation only made him worse. His conduct was at times fiend-like; fifteen times has he turned me out doors, thrice in my night clothes. Many, many times has he struck at me with whatever he could lay hold of. Once he attempted to kill me with a hatchet. He often punished the children severely for nothing, and once he would have thrown the youngest out of a second-story window if I had not prevented him.

"In the midst of all this, whenever he showed me any kind-ness, or smiled as he was once wont to do, it was like balm to my wounded heart, and it brought back the recollection of the first happy months of our espousals. The hope that he might reform never wholly forsook me, and it would revive with all its brightness at such times. This, and the thought that he was the father of my children made me cling to him in the midst of all his neglect and cruelty.

In his younger days, he had bought a snug little place. He took no care of it, and it gradually got into a very bad state. It was mortgaged to the licensed rum-seller that I have before alluded to, and at length went into his possession. This very man has refused to trust me for flour and potatoes, while he was at the same time every day selling rum to my husband, without any limit but that of his burning appetite. He now occupies that home of which he robbed me by plotting in cool blood the ruin of my husband, and all under the *guise* of law. This despoiler of my home still holds up his head in society, and still has the license of law for his horrid business.

"Mr. Rawley at last broke his skull by falling from a building, and died. Then anguish came upon me, equalled only by that first bitter draught of the cup of sorrow, when I was for the first time convinced of his evil habits. Now the hope which had clung to me through all, was utterly gone; the husband of my bosom I could now think of only as having that destiny *unalterably* fastened on him which the Bible, with awful certainty, declares to be the everlasting portion of the drunkard."

'The other females in that room I can notice but slightly. That slip-shod, shiftless old lady, Mrs. Barlow, that sits there with no other business than to tend her snuff box, has an only son, who was for many years a taverner, then a licensed retailer, and now a drunkard of the worst type. Mrs. Jennings, who sits by her in friendly chat, is the widow of a notorious old sot. Her troubles have affected her very differently from Mrs. Rawley. She is discontented, peevish and jealous, asking for the pity and condolence of every body, and always trying to cry by way of emphasis to her tale of woe, but never able to squeeze out a single tear. She is constantly quarrelling with Mrs. Jones, a slouching, bold-looking woman, the opposite side of the room. Mrs. J. was once the wife of a rum-seller, and she became one of the earliest victims of his business. Since his death she has been a wanderer, and one of the vilest pests of society, and she occasionally finds a resting place in the Alms-House. When she came there last, she had pawned nearly all her clothes to a rum-seller. She was one of the associates, of Rawley in the depth of his degradation, and so poor Mrs. Rawley has to suffer sadly from the bitings of her tongue, but she bears it all patiently. "'Tis all for the best," said Mrs. Rawley one day, in relation to some trouble. "Humph," said the peevish Mrs. Jennings, "I don't b'leive in taking every thing so quietly." "What a pretty little saint friend Rawley's widow is," said Mrs. Jones, with an oath.

Such are the companions of this lovely, excellent woman. On whom rests the guilt of putting her in such companionship? Chiefly on *unauthorized agent of the law*, the rum-seller who made her husband the victim of his cupidity, and in cold blood consummated his ruin, and drove his suffering family from their home to make way for himself. O, when will our legislators forbear to give their sanction to such outrages as this? The license law is a disgrace to the statute book, and the voice of multitudes of women ground down to the dust, cries to you to tear it out.

I will continue my sketches next week.

P. S. We had a drunken row here a night or two since. Some rum was smuggled into the house. It was brought by Capt. Pepper's hopeful son, who came to make his loving father a call. Whether it was bought of a licensed rum-seller I don't know; but at any rate, it made drunk come. Mr. Babcock has put Capt. Pepper, Old Dilly, and the vixen Mrs. Jones in close confinement.

Another thing occurred which I must mention. "Crazy Flint," a good natured crazy fellow that wanders about your streets, found an old man that had run away and got drunk, and led him back to the Alms-House. He was a little staggering himself, and as he led the old man in, said he, M Humph, Mr. Babcock; the blind leading the blind, but we didn't fall into the ditch. We saw some other folks on the way that came near it, though. They were gentlemen—been to some celebration, I s'pose—*genteelly* drunk—that is, drunk on wine —knees like Belshazzar's knees—was a good mind to complain of them to some justice and bring them along with this old fellow— but it wouldn't do—gentlemen you know—*genteelly* drunk!"

Yours, &c.

LETTER VI.

DEAR SIR,

I will now give you some brief sketches of my male associates in the Alms-House.

Mr. Wheaton, an easy sort of man, easily influenced either to good or evil, was once a merchant. His friends were of the first respectability, and they made many efforts to reform him, but all in vain. At one time he, however, abstained for nearly a year from every kind of alcoholic drink, at which his friends, and especially his poor wife, greatly rejoiced. At length he happened to be a little dyspeptic, and a seller of wine and beer (it is said he sometimes sells something stronger,) prepared some wine bitters for him which he said would certainly cure him. This was the beginning of his back-sliding, and he soon became worse than ever. Of course he failed in his business, and his family became poor, and were supported by their friends. His wife died broken-hearted. She belonged to the same church with the seller of beer and wine, and often heard him pray, but with feelings of anguish, for she never thought of him but as the destroyer of her husband.

Mr. Clary was once a retailer, and he knows all the secrets of the trade. He was set up in business by a wholesale dealer; and here I would remark that all the talk of wholesale dealers against dram-selling (for they are inconsistent enough to deal out their homilies on this subject to temperance men) is perfectly hypocrit-ical; for whatever their professions may be, they know that they supply the dirty dram-sellers, who are really their agents to distrib-ute the liquid fire through the community. Mr. Clary at first had a license, but as many of his neighbours sold without one and were not molested, he concluded it was useless for him to pay his five dollars for the privilege of making people drunk when it could be enjoyed without this tax. I asked him if he thought that when he sold rum under the authority of law it affected people any better than it did when he sold it without authority—"that is, in your experience, is getting 'drunk by law' any better than getting drunk against the law?" "It's about the same thing," said he, laughing. "Well," said I, "I thought so too; but our legislators make a difference for some reason or other, for they appoint drunkard-makers of ' their own, and forbid under penalty the making, of drunkards by any body else, as if the business of drunkard-making could not be properly done by any one except their agents. But you think you made drunkards as *skillfully* without a license as you did with one?" "Yes; the rum made drunk come as quick in the one case as in the other," said he.

Mr. C was a very good-natured well-disposed man when not under the influence of rum—so he was very communicative to me. He said that his conscience was often troubled, especially when he saw the evil effects which resulted from the liquor which he sold. But he had at hand the numberless excuses which are in every rum-seller's mouth, to silence his conscience; and if these failed to do it, there was a never-failing quietus which he would resort to—that was rum. Rum-selling, in other words drunkard-making, he said, was a very profitable business, if the seller could keep from making a drunkard of himself. But that Mr. Clary could not do; the temptation being always before his eyes, often overcame him. He at length became a notorious drunkard, and his establishment was transferred to another hopeful satellite of the wholesale dealer. This same respectable wholesale dealer took even his pigs from Mr. C., though he knew that his wife had bought them with the fruits of her own industry, and had the whole care of them herself. After this Mr. C. became worse and worse, and was a constant torment to his family. A short time since he got very angry because his wife had hid his bottle from him, and he at once began to break the furniture. He demolished the crockery oh her shelves, turned over the tea table, scalding his youngest child terribly, and struck his wife down with a chair; he-had done similar things before, and *every rum seller in town knew it*, and yet this man never had any difficulty in buying rum. At this very time he got his rum of a licensed retailer, and "was drunk by authority of the State of Connecticut!"

We pass to another case, Wilson is a frank generous sailor, the only son of a pious widow. He lately came in from sea, and as his pockets were full of money, the dram-sellers marked him for a prize, and they have picked him well. Though he has been here hut three weeks, they have managed to get hold of all his money. He was very much injured in a drunken row at a grog-shop, and was brought to the Alms-House to be taken care of. He is a fellow of superior natural abilities and has a vein of fine humour, so that his conversation is very amusing, and we have had many pleasant hours together. He said he had been a wild fellow, he hardly knew why, and he hoped his good mother's prayers in his behalf would be some time or other answered. Whenever he spoke of his mother the tear would glisten in his eye, and his lips would tremble with the effort to suppress his rising feelings. Perhaps the next moment he would utter some remark at which neither of us could help laughing through our tears. A knot of us would sometimes get around him to hear his yarns, and then you might see a laughable scene. At every good point of the story, Old Dilly would have his usual response ready, "that's grammatically spoken," and Captain Pepper would open his great gulfing orifice under his big red nose, out of which would issue a thundering ha! ha! ha! the rest of the company echoing it.

Last Saturday was a very rainy day, and we all worked in the house, picking oakum. We had a little temperance discussion, and it was rather more lively than such discussions commonly are. Capt. Pepper said that he thought it was good to drink a little, and that he himself had never been in the habit of drinking *much*. "Enough, however, to give you a red nose," said I. " That's owing to a kind of 'sipelas humour in my blood, that my mother said I was always troubled with," said he. "More likely," said Wilson, "a sipping humour, or a humour for sipping, which is in your brain instead of your blood. Your mother was probably very correct in saying that you was always troubled with it." "That's grammatically spoken," said Dilly. "Well, you needn't all go to running foul of my big nose, for it has nothing to do with the subject we were talking about." "I think it has a good deal to. do with it, Captain," said Wilson, "and it's not out of order at all; for I contend a red nose is pretty plain evidence of drinking. It's as plain as a man's nose on his face, as we say." "Well," said the Captain, "I don't care; I know I never have been drunk many times, and I believe there's such a thing as a man's controlling himself without putting his name down to a paper." "That's grammatically spoken," said Old Dilly, throwing down a handful of oakum by way of emphasis. " Everybody," continued he of the red nose, "ought to have the liberty to do as he pleases. I don't believe in being led by the priests and tied to women's apron strings." "I 'gree with you 'zactly," said a stupid-looking fellow, who had quarrelled with his wife for years, and had recently left her. "And so do I," said Wilson, "I think the right to get drunk is one of the inalienable rights, and the priests and the women have combined to take this right away from us jolly fellows." "I didn't say any thing," said the Captain, "about the right to *get drunk*. You are always making fun of what I say, Wilson. I said that every man had a right to *drink* if he pleased." "It's the same thing," said Wilson. "The way to get drunk is to drink—that's my way, isn't it yours, Captain? I beg your pardon. I should have said, wasn't it your way the *very few* times that you say you have got drunk in your lifetime?" Captain Pepper looked rather angry and I was afraid that there would be an end to the sport, so I pretended to take his part. He soon got a going again. "I don't like this *binding* ourselves; its taking away our liberties." "The liberty to get drunk, you mean—excuse me—the liberty to drink, I should say," said Wilson. "I believe," continued the Captain, "that a man is a great deal more apt to drink when he has bound himself not to; it makes him hanker after it most dreadfully; it's like forbidden fruit, you know." "Yes," added Wilson, "and a man is a great deal more apt to pay what he owes his neighbour if he don't give him his note for it, and he is more apt to be a faithful husband to his wife if he has never gone through that *binding* process of taking the marriage vow." Captain Pepper stared at Wilson, and hardly seemed to know what to say to this. I started a new topic. "These Cold-water men are rather hard on the rum sellers, don't you think so, Captain?" "Yes, and it's too bad," said he. "It's a lawful business, and I think our Gineral 'Sembly wouldn't sanction it if it wasn't right." "They are certainly very wise men," said I, "and they have provided very amply for those who prize the liberty of getting drunk. A man can get drunk by law, and be taken care of snugly by law after he is drunk." "I'll tell you a story on that," said Wilson. "I once got drunk on some rum sold to me by a grand juror's clerk, whereupon I was rather noisy in the street. The grand juror himself came along just at this time, and rebuked me. I told him it was his rum that made me act so, at which he was very angry, and he complained of me to a rum-selling Justice. I was delivered over to a rum-selling constable, to be carried to the work-house. Well, we Stopped on the road to get something to drink. The constable got so drunk that he sat down by the road-side and went to sleep. I had just then a little rather go to the work-house than not—so I took the mittimus[11] out of his pocket, and went on to the alms-house, acting as my own constable. This was what I call a very consistent legal rum transaction—a rum law well executed by rum agents."

I have not time nor space to give any more of this discussion, nor to describe any more of my interesting associates. Next week you shall have my own history.

P.S. I have told some very hard things about the rum-sellers in this place. Why have they not made a rumpus about it? Not because they are such a good-natured set, most certainly; nor because they think their traffic is above reproach. It is simply because they can make no sort of defence, and the stiller they keep the better it is for them. They would be glad enough to choke "that Alms-House fellow" off, if it could be done quietly; and one of them did tell Mr. Babcock that he had better pay me something "*to leave town*" as your beautifully *concise* town accounts express it, and even offered to pay the sum himself.

Yours, &c.

---

11   [Latin, we send] mittimus: a warrant issued to a sheriff commanding the delivery to prison of a person named in the warrant. Archaic and obsolete legal term.

LETTER No. VII.

DEAR SIR,

I will now, agreeably to the promise I made last week, relate my history.

I have said that I was from a noble family. My name is John Cotton Mather, and I am of the stock of Mather of Magnalia memory.[12] With such noble blood in my veins, I was not to be conquered by so mean an enemy as Rum. No; it was the *refined, the classic God of Wine*, whose praises have been sung by poets, and proclaimed by philosophers, that first overcame me—though of late it has been ungenteel, vulgar New England Rum that has held me as its easy prey. At fifteen years, of age I entered College. My moral character was then without a stain. I was the pride of my father, and the joy of my mother. O! how has that pride been humbled, and that joy been destroyed! I was unsuspecting and knew nothing of the wiles of the world, so that temptation easily overcame me. Wine-drinking was then a general custom in College; so much so, that a professor of religion might drink to the borders of intoxication, nay, even to intoxication itself, and be looked upon as committing, at most, but a very venial sin. I will not detail the steps by which I became a drunkard. That horrid result was arrived at in a little less than two years, and I was dismissed from College at length, on account of repeated find gross intoxication.[13] My father tried various plans to reform me, but in vain. As a last resort, he sent me off upon a whaling voyage.[14] Upon our return we were shipwrecked, and-after suffering many hardships, I at last reached home. Vice had not yet destroyed my natural sensibilities, and the hardships I had endured had revived them in their original energy.

---

12   The Mather family were founding stock, Puritan clergy, in New England. They were involved in the Salem witch trials.
13   Big Book, pg. 172-173, "After many painful discussions, they finally gave me my credits and I migrated to another of the leading universities of the country and entered as a Junior that fall."
14   Moby Dick was published in 1851. Entirely possible that Melville read this narrative. He has colorful remarks on Temperance Societies.

A Reformed Drunkard

As I entered my father's house, a poor weather-beaten sailor, I wept like a child, and as my parents and brothers and sisters gathered around me to greet me, I was speechless. As my father that night, before the evening altar, thanked God that the "lost was found," in the fulness of my feelings I resolved that I would wander no more, and that temptation should be resisted to the death.

For a year I tasted not even a drop of wine, though it was then made use of (it being long before the temperance effort was begun) as the common social beverage in the highest circles of society. I had not only my own appetite to resist, but the sparkling wine was continually before me. After a while, getting tired of being singular, the whole mass of society being in practice against me, I ventured to taste, and though a few, a very few, whispered the word, beware, in my ear, most of my friends did not seem to think that I was treading on dangerous ground, and as I was pleased to find that I could indulge myself without going beyond the bounds of mod-eration, I became less and less cautious. I was, however, for a long time free from actual intoxication. My father put me into mercan-tile business with an older partner, and in a few months after I was married to one of the most beautiful and lovely girls in the town. I was now most happily situated—in business with one of the best of men, surrounded with many friends, and above all, blessed with an excellent and lovely wife—but, reader, I was a *Wine Drinker*, There was near by a shop in which were sold Confectionery, Oysters, Wine, &c. There was a back room fitted up for an eating-room, and this was a common place of resort for young men. The most steady, and even the religious were occasionally seen there, so that I felt no scruple as to the propriety of going there also. But my visits were more and more frequent, and once in a while I would go home from them, to say the least, unnaturally excited. My wife at first with tears remonstrated with me, and my partner and other friends did the same. This would do some good for a little time, but I was fairly within the current of the whirlpool, and in spite of the efforts put forth to save me, the circling flood was carrying me nearer and nearer to its centre with awful certainty. I soon wholly neglected my business, and my partner, after bearing with me with the patience of a father, dissolved his connexon with me. My father, after this,

31

continued to find some employment of one kind or another for me; but though I would at times behave very well for a month or two, on the whole I was getting worse and worse. My wife lost all her bloom, and became thin and haggard. I saw it—I knew what was the cause—but though I loved her as I loved my own soul, I loved the wine cup more. She was gradually worn out by her troubles, and at length sickened and died. As that sweet spirit was going to heaven, I promised her with tears that I would repent and forsake my sins. Yet the very night after her burial I got intoxicated, and because I could find nothing else in the house to do it with, I took a bottle of Cologne that I found in her chamber. From that time I have been a wanderer. Occasionally I have been to my father's house, where I have always been welcomed with affection, notwithstanding all the evil that I have done. Hope has again and again been lighted up in the bosom, and they have made unwearied efforts to reform me; but I was an easy prey to temptation, and soon relapsed. I have been miserable, and have for years known nothing of happiness. My chains have galled me, and yet I have clung to them.

Such is the history of a wine drinker. Many of my companions who used to frequent that *respectable* eating shop have run a similar course. We there *began* a course of preparation for the vile and filthy scenes of the vulgar grog-shop. I would, therefore, warn every visiter of such a shop to beware, lest he take the first step in the downward road of intemperance. The drinker of wine, and ale, and cordials runs no small risk of becoming at length the besotted victim of rum. I would echo the solemn warning of the Bible—"Look not thou upon the wine when it is red;" for I can testify that "at the last it biteth like a serpent and stingeth like an adder."[15]

One word more. I wish not to detract from the guilt which rests upon me, yet I verily believe that I should have succeeded in that first attempt at reformation, which I made after my return from sea, if the customs of society had not been wholly opposed to my efforts. There were in my case all the incentives that could possibly exist, to prompt me to a course of virtue ; my business was pros-

15   Proverbs 23:32

perous; I had a numerous circle of the best of friends around me; my natural qualities were such as to fit me to receive and impart enjoyment to a high degree in social intercourse; and the wife of my bosom was one who could exert almost the influence of a guardian angel; but all these were not adequate to withstand the influence of the *social* cup, addressing itself as it did at every step, with its bewitching allurements, to a propensity which had gathered strength by years of indulgence.

Next week I shall give you a few thoughts on the License Law, and then I shall be done.

Yours, &c.

LETTER No. VIII.

DEAR SIR,

I HAVE now done with my Alms-House sketches, and I will conclude with some brief remarks on that masterpiece of unjust, and I may add, ridiculous legislation—the License Law.

Though we daily witness much intemperance, the temperance reformation which has been going on for the last twelve years, has affected an astonishing change in the community. Twelve years ago, alcoholic drink was the common beverage among all classes; but now its use is very generally discarded in all good society, and this is no small change. But the change is not an *universal* one. It is very much confined to the *reflecting* portion of the community, to those who have some weight of character to enable them to resist any evil influences to which they may be exposed. But there is a mass of loose materials, having no fixed character, existing in every community, that have as yet been acted upon very partially by the temperance reformation. I refer to that lower class of society, that have no settled character, nor habits, nor employment, but whose course is shaped altogether by accidental circumstances. It is this class that now furnishes most, perhaps we may say nearly all, the recruits to the ranks of the drunkards. They are men who, after their work for the day is over, or in fact at any time when they are idle, (and this is often,) are disposed to lounge about wherever they can find companions to their taste. Rum-shops, from the decent shop of the licensed retailer, down to the dirtiest grog-shop, are their common places of rendezvous. It is here that multitudes of young men are running the drunkard's race and are preparing to inflict distress on their friends and families, and to fill at length our prisons and alms-houses. Here are the fountains of three-fourths of the vice and pauperism in the land. Here is the chief obstacle to the complete triumph of temperance.

What course, let us ask, ought legislators to take in relation to this evil? What course does justice require? Is it *just* that these nurseries of crime and pauperism should be protected, nay, established by law? Who are benefited by this traffic? Certainly not the drunkard, who is ruined by it, body, soul, and estate; nor his family, who suffer from his neglect—perhaps his cruelty; nor the community upon whom this traffic inflicts such an amount of evil, in the shape of pauperism and crime. Who, then, are benefited by it? None bitt that small portion of the community who are engaged in this traffic. Was there ever a more unjust monopoly? Here is a set of men following a business which produces at least three-fourths of all the evils that exist in society. Is it *just* that they should be permitted to do this? Have we not a right, on the common principles of *self-protection*, to claim that such a business should be viewed by the law as a crime, and treated as a crime? And yet the law not only allows, but sanctions this business. Drunkenness, in the face of all decency and justice, is legalized among us. The Bible, the only true text book of justice and law, pronounces a woe upon him that maketh his neighbour drunken; but our wise legislators have taken the responsibility of contradicting the Bible, and grant a *plenary indulgence* to those who pay five dollars into the treasury. Yes, for this pitiful sum they permit a man to deluge |he community with crime and pauperism. I ask again, is this to be submitted to? Have we not a right to protect ourselves against such an enormous evil?

The right is claimed and allowed in regard to other evils—for example, lottery dealing and gambling. But the traffic in ardent spirits is ten-fold, nay, a hundred-fold more productive of injury to society than these evils are. And if it is the duty of legislators to protect the community against them, then it is a vastly more imperative duty to protect it against this traffic. The drunkard has a right to this protection. I can speak feelingly on this subject. The *drunkard* is the prey of the rum-seller; though he be guilty, the rum-seller who coolly makes money out of his ruin is more guilty than he is. Ought not then the arm of the law to be put forth to rescue the poor victim of the rum-seller's avarice? The *family* of the drunkard have a right to this protection. The rum-seller is truly their enemy, their oppressor. He gets his livelihood by turning their natural protector into a monster, and sending him home to them at night, to inflict upon them abuse and cruelty. The whole *community* have a right to this protection; for it is injured, deeply injured by this traffic. It is taxed by it with an enormous bill of expense, and its peace and happiness, and prosperity are sadly wounded by it.

Does not all this commend itself to every man's judgment and conscience? And yet you quietly permit *forty* grog-shops in this place, to be pouring poverty, crime, disease, and death over the face of this community? Are the friends of temperance asleep? If the evil be as great as it is said to be, is it not their duty to arouse, and never cease their efforts till the law shall be so framed, that you can rid yourselves of this greatest evil that exists in society. Look at the tax which the rum-sellers lay upon you in the single item of pauperism. The support of your poor costs you annually $2000. Three-fourths of this, $1500, is the result of the grog-shop system. How much of this amount comes back to you? Only $40; for but *eight* out of the forty rum sellers in this place have taken out a license. Here then is a set of men who pay you $40 for the privilege of taxing you $1500. Is this just? Have you not a right to rid yourselves of such a tax? Taxes are not commonly quietly submitted to, if there be even a *suspicion* that they are useless or unjust. Why then is there such an apathy in relation to a tax, the injustice of which is undisputed?

I have exposed in some of my letters the glaring, and I may say *laughable* inconsistencies of the License Law. And it is because these inconsistencies are so palpable, that the penalties existing against selling without a license are so seldom executed. The public see and feel that drunkard-making is just as criminal when done under the authority of a license, as when it is done without this authority. Let a law be constructed which is based upon the principles of justice, and I am persuaded that public sentiment is strong enough to secure its faithful execution. If this community could say by the ballot-box whether rum-selling should be licensed or not, I believe there would be a strong vote against it. Every town ought to have the right to do this. The law is framed after this plan in Massachusetts, and works well—so well, that the rum-party have made a desperate effort to get it altered, but in vain. I will mention one fact to show how well the law is executed. In one county there were collected in fines $1200 in one year—more, I will venture to say, than has been collected in the whole State of Connecticut for breaches of the License Law for five years past.

Some pretend to think that public sentiment alone, unassisted by law, is adequate to destroy intemperance. But I can tell them, from what I have seen of rum-sellers in my career of intemperance, that, as a body of men, they care not for public sentiment, and that nothing but the strong arm of the law can reach them. Little do they care for what is said about them in the public prints, or in the speeches of temperance men, so long as they are left to go on unmolested in their business. The man who can, for the sake of gain, deliberately scatter poverty, crime, disease, and death around him, has so steeled his heart and benumbed his conscience, that he can confront the whole community with a brazen face. If the misery which he produces in the community in a thousand forms cannot affect his heart, how can you expect that he will heed the opinions of his fellow men 1 If he is deaf to the cry of the widow and the orphan, whose property, whose happiness have been sacrificed to his cruel avarice, how can he be otherwise than deaf to the voice of public sentiment? Oh, the rum-seller is as cruel as the grave; misery is all about his path, and he *knows* it; say what he will, he *knows* it; and yet he will go in this abominable traffic. Nothing but the force of *law* can stay his hand from his deadly work.

I have done. I hope that I have effected some good in giving my sketches to the public. My sixty days, for which I was sentenced to the work-house, are gone, and I take respectful leave of my company for the present.

Yours, &c.

PART II.

RECOLLECTIONS.

BY THE AUTHOR OF "LETTERS FROM THE ALMS-HOUSE."

A Reformed Drunkard

No. I.

IT is now near four years since I left the Alms-House in Norwich, in which I wrote those letters. I left it wretched, ragged, and I was about to say friendless. I had, how-ever, friends to whom I could go—friends who recollected me in years past, when they esteemed me as a man and loved me as a friend. And although the efforts which they had so many times made for my reformation had proved fruitless, yet I had no doubt that they were ready to help me again. I had too an aged father and mother, whose gray hairs I had nearly brought with sorrow to the grave. Like the prodigal in the gospel, I resolved to go to my father's house. I knew that I should be forgiven and welcomed, though I had been for years a wretch and a wanderer. And it was so. It was just at dusk that I stood at the back door of a neat farm-house in one of the loveliest spots on this earth. Every thing around looked nearly as it did when in the bright days of boyhood this was the scene of my sports. There stood the same old well whose cold water had so often refreshed me, and as my eye fell upon it I sighed as I thought of the worse than broken cisterns that I had hewed out to myself since I had been a wanderer ; and the aspiration rose in my heart that henceforth my parched lips should find refreshment only at this well of water, and that my withered, desolate soul should draw here the living waters from the well of salvation. I aed at the door, and a man bowed down with age opened it. It was my father. I was so changed that in the dimness of twilight, he did not recognize me. I thought that I would not make myself known at once, so I asked for food, and he bade me walk in; for it was not his custom to send the hungry traveller, however ragged and filthy he might be, away unsupplied from his door. My good old mother placed some food on a table, as I had often seen her do in my boyhood for just such wandering wretches as I now was. She lighted a candle, and as she set it down she cast upon me the glance of curiosity, and then it seemed as if her eye were fastened upon me as by a spell. At length some expression of my countenance in a twinkling dispelled the mystery, and she exclaimed, It is, it is my son; and the next moment, even in my rags, I received their warm embrace. I told them my story, and we wept together, I, tears of gratitude and revived affection, and they, tears of joy and hope, and forgiving love.

The next day I appeared in the streets of my native village, clothed and in my right mind, the wonder of all who saw me. Some greeted me kindly and shook me by the hand as an old friend; but in many I saw the cold look of distrust—that look which has driven many a drunkard back to his cups when he had fully resolved to reform. The Baltimore reformers are teaching temperance men a good practical lesson on tins point, and the adverse circumstances which have always stood in the way of the drunkard's reformation are beginning to be removed.

I remained at home a few months, employing myself in taking care of the garden and doing whatever needed to be done in the every day routine of the family. I was not contented with this; I wished for something more to do. As 1 was a good penman, 1 at length succeeded in getting a place in the large town of W—as a nook-keeper. I obtained here the favour not only of my employers, but of the community around me. Every thing went on smoothly for three months. Appetite was often strong, sometimes almost overwhelming, but I succeeded in resisting it. I was always of a social turn, and therefore ready to mingle in the social pleasures of society, and of course to partake in the festivities generally connected with them. And here lay the temptation which first overcame me. The annual agricultural fair was attended by every body; and I was one of the gazing and delighted multitude. I was urged by a companion to go to the public dinner which was got up on the occasion; I did so. There I saw clergymen who preach about the horrors of intemperance; magistrates who sit in judgment upon the poor drunkard; and worthy citizens who had joined the temperance society, all drinking a vile compound called wine,—the vulgar, ungenteel rum of the grog-shop so dragged as to have the taste and colour of the pure juice of the grape,—the worm of the still was there, but with his court dress on, a red coat to please his refined and moral and religious company. With his homespun one on he would have been frowned down and trodden under foot. When the toasts were drank, I filled my glass with water. I saw that I was observed, but felt firmly resolved to drink no wine. At length a jovial fellow opposite to me said to me as a very witty toast was announced, "Mather, that's too good a toast to pour cold water on to," at the same time filling up my glass from the decanter. Amid the roar of laughter, in which I joined as heartily as any one, I sipped. It was but a sip, thought I, and that too of wine and water, for there was some (a little, it is true,) water in my glass when he poured in the wine. It was thus I calmed down the risings of my conscience.

The first sip is often the first step in the pathway to destruction. "C'est premier pas qui conte," as the French proverb has it.[16] The reformed man who would perhaps be shocked at the idea of drinking down a full glass of wine, seeing in it the opening course of ruin, sees not the same danger from a sip, especially if it be half water. A mere sip seems nothing, and yet it is often enough to waken up the old appetite from its slumber. Besides, the sip, having been taken apparently with impunity, leads to another and another, till enough is taken to dizzen and excite the head, and then the work is done. The beginnings of evil or of good, moral or physical, are usually small. The germ that bursts from the seed is but a little germ. The stream, that bears on its bosom the mighty ships, or sweeps along a torrent to destroy, began a mere dozing of a drop, and tributaries were ready on every hand to join it and make it what it is. These are "old saws" but not " old wives fables." The world is scarred all over with evidences of their truth. Reader, if you are a reformed drunkard or a moderate drinker, beware, lest your ruin prove them true.

That evening I went home drunk, and the next morning I was sick. One of my employers came to see me, as I supposed to give me my discharge. In this I was mistaken* It was fortunate for me that I got drunk in good company* It would not look very consistent for him to turn me off, while he, in common with the whole

16   Mme. du Deffand describes, in a letter to Horace Walpole, June 6, 1767, the origin of one of the most celebrated *mots* in the French language. She says that Cardinal de Polignac, who was a great talker, and a man of extraordinary credulity, had given her an account of the martyrdom of St. Denis at Montmartre, and stated that, after his decapitation, he walked with his head in his hands, two leagues to the spot where afterwards the cathedral dedicated to him was built, in the village called by his name. Her comment was, "The distance is nothing: it is only the first step that costs" (La distance n'y fait rien: il n'y a que le premier pas qui coûte).

community received as freely as ever into fellowship the respectable lawyer, and the three respectable merchants, who were as drunk as I was. So he gave me a lecture, and told me he would try me longer. In my next I will continue my history to its consummation in my perfect reform.

Yours, &c.

No. II

I CAME near having another downfall at a wedding, where the clergyman himself, a grave D. D., set the example of drinking wine, (or red rum,) with the remark that he liked such weddings as they had in Cana of Galilee. This was applauded by a general hum from most of the company. With this license from so high a source as a "legate of the skies," I, urged on by appetite, should have certainly drank, had not some sensible remarks fallen from the lips of a young man sitting near me, who ventured to ask the clergyman, very much to his confusion, whether he supposed that the wine offered to the present company was such as our Saviour drank at the marriage in Cana.

This "word in season" encouraged me to resist my appetite and refuse the wine. The confusion of the clergyman was but for a moment, and he replied with an air of contempt and easy indifference, "Wine is wine—nothing more orthodox than wine at weddings," and turning to the father of the bride, to which he of course nodded assent, remarking, very sagely, that some people were wise above what is written. This theological Goliath, thought I, is a little afraid of the cold-water arguments, the "stones *out of the brook*" which this young David has in readiness to sling at him. One young man, who said with an oath, that Parson Clark was a fine liberal fellow, and no cold-water fanatic, was drunk when the party broke up, and several others who applauded his remark, got at least to the point of silliness. And the next day, as a knot of young men were standing in front of our shop, there came up one who was a sort of oracular wit among them, and said, "Well, fellows, these *Galilean* weddings, eh, first rate," at which there was a great shout. A conversation followed of the most blasphemous character. Would that Parson Clark could have heard it.

One day there came into our shop a Mr. Draper, who once kept a grog-shop in Norwich, and had just opened one a stone's throw from us. I was once for a little time the oracle, the ringleader of his shop—" the old hen of the brood," as Hawkins has it. He was surprised to see me—so different from the bloated, ragged creature that I was when his customer. He greeted me, but rather distantly. Some one soon said something about temperance, at which he sneered. I indignantly rebuked him. I could not help it, for 1 knew him to have under his fair exterior the heart of a fiend—a heart that could coldly plot the ruin of his fellow-man for the sake of dollars and cents, and I *had been his victim*. He was made pale and trembling by my rebuke, but in return taunted me about my former habits. "I know it all," said I, "I know that I have been a drunkard, and you know that I was once in your clutches, and you were pushing me down to ruin, body and soul, and for what? for a little money. But, thank God, I have thrown off your chains." And so I went on to pour it into him, until he, seeing that I had the sympathy of the bystanders, slinked off like a whipped dog. Rum-sellers can stand any thing better than the fire of reformed drunkards, even when it is but a single fire—how will they stand a whole park of artillery brought to bear upon them by an army of such men as are now rallying round the standard which Mitchell and Hawkins first hoisted in Baltimore!

I had not yet done with Mr. Draper. As I passed by his shop one morning, I recognized in the door an old acquaintance, Wilson, the generous- hearted sailor, who, the reader will recollect, was with me in the Alms-House at Norwich.

His hat was canted to one side in his usual waggish manner, and he had the same playful countenance that he used to have when talking with Captain Pepper and old Dilly. I at once accosted him, but I was so changed that he did not know me. But when he found who I was he gave me a hearty welcome. He stepped out of the door, for he saw by my dress and appearance that Mr. Draper's shop was now no place of my choice. I found that he had just returned from a short cruise, and had come to W— with a shipmate who lived there. He had been in town only a few days, but Mr. Draper had succeeded in getting most of his money by such means as dram-sellers well understand. He had been on a regular spree, and Mr. Draper's shop was his headquarters. It was very easy to take a five dollar bill from him for a one, when Wilson was intoxicated, or to make wrong change in various ways, or, if need be, he could put his hand into Wilson's pocket when he was in the depth of his drunken sleep. In no other way could Wilson account for the loss of so much money. When I saw him he had taken one glass to remove his morning exhaustion produced by the last night's debauch, and Mr. Draper was preparing him another. I persuaded him to go with me, and he went into the shop and laid three cents on the counter saying, "take that but your rum I don't want I have had enough of it, and you have had enough of my money. Good-bye, sir." We left him cursing "that cold-water rascal, Mather," as rum-sellers are wont to curse any one who plucks a victim from their murderous fangs.

Well, Wilson was delivered for the time being, but how could I keep him out of danger. I succeeded in getting him place as a truck-man for one of our merchants, a strong temperance man. A sailor is always rather awkward in managing a horse at first, but Wilson soon learned to make him mind his helm, and became quite attached to his new employment. Here I leave him to go on with my own story. The reader shall know more of him anon.

One of the partners in our shop, a young man of great promise, as a business man and as a citizen, was in the habit of going often to a very genteel confectionery. It would have disgraced him to have been seen drinking rum in a dram-shop, but he could drink *the same rum drugged so as to look and taste like wine*, and ale, Taylor's Albany ale perchance, in a confectionery, to which even strong temperance men resort for refreshment. The truth is, these confectioneries prepare victims for the vulgar dram-shop. And there are different grades of them to suit all sorts of customers, from the splendid establishment with rooms for ladies, where nothing but (*ah, that nothing but*) wine, and porter, and ale are sold, and from which the intoxicated man would be kicked out, (that is unless he were one of the gentility—then he would be led home and the matter be hushed up,) down to the low shop where any and all the forms of intoxicating liquors can be had by any body, however ragged, or dirty, or filthy, or drunk, he may be.

Let every reformed man beware of such shops, for they are the most dangerous traps which lie along his path. The danger of going to a dram-shop is palpable, but not so with confectioneries, As you look into them, you would not dream that the dominions of Alcohol extended there, amidst all this array of delicacies, and the fruits of the earth. The evil is partially *concealed.* The beginnings of *drunkenness* are here so masked by fascinating accompaniments, that many begin here their course of ruin without being aware of their danger, and many, who had escaped the toils of the tyrant Alcohol, are here again drawn into them gently, often, but most surely and sometimes fatally.

Though I felt for some time that it would be hazardous for me to go to the confectionery frequented by my esteemed employer, his example gradually overcame my fears. After exerting myself one day strongly at a fire, I passed directly by this shop on my return, and as others went in to get some refreshment I went in with them. And as those with whom I chanced to go in asked for some ale, the keeper of the shop poured me out a tumbler also, supposing me to be one- of their company.

How powerful the influence of mere circumstances! If I had been obliged to ask for the ale myself, I should not have drank it, but as it was placed before me, my appetite formed an easy excuse in the disagreeableness of a refusal, and though I resolved that it should be but one tumbler, appetite was so thoroughly roused that I took another and another, and then went to a confectionery of a lower order where I drank myself beastly drunk. Here my friend Wilson found me at evening and led me home. The next day, the senior partner in our shop came to see me. At first he was much inclined to reproach me, but after hearing my whole story he pitied me. He solemnly warned me, as my only ground of safety, never again to step over the *threshold even* of any shop where alcohol in *any guise* is sold. When the other partner learned what license 1 had taken from his example, he showed at once that he was a conscientious and benevolent man, by resolving that he would no longer stand in the way of the reformation of a fellowman. From this time he ceased to frequent the confectioner's shop, and honestly told him his reasons for so doing, at the same time beseeching him to banish the drunkard's drink in every shape from his establishment. The appeal, however, was in vain; money, *money*, that "root of all evil"[17] was in the way. His plea for his course was that the public would not support a *dry-shop* as he termed it. He said, too, that the *little* that he sold of wine or ale could do no harm. "Did not," said my friend, "the ale that you sold the other day to our clerk, Mather, do harm?" "He did not get drunk at my shop," was the reply. "True, he did not get so as actually to stagger on the ale you sold him, but it was only a little short of it, And then, he *began*, mark that, he began at your shop a course which, in a few hours, ended in beastly drunkenness at your neighbour's shop. And here is the evil, of such shops. Many of the young men who go to them learn here the *first lesson* of the drunkard. Besides," continued he, "they are a part of one grand system for the making of drunkards. The respectable young lawyer, or merchant, or clerk, will, of course keep away from a groggery—*his* strong drink he must get in a more genteel form than rum, and a more genteel place than a dram-shop—so genteel that ladies can go there. *And commonly something stronger can be drunk in some parts of the shop than in others.* The ladies may see nothing of the wine and ale, and especially of the whisky punch, and the staid temperance man, that comes in to the front part of the shop to buy some delicious fruit, or to drink a glass of soda, may see nothing of them, though is son may be within the walls of that establishment, gulping them down at the very same time." The confectioner could stand no longer the home-thrusts of his quondam patron, and with trembling lips he asked him, "How is it that you have become so wise and conscientious all at once?" "Mather's case has revealed to me the truth," replied he. "My esteem for him, and my desire for his confirmed reformation, have led me to think of this subject as I have never thought of it before. I thought it my duty to tell you the conclusion that I had come to, with my reason for it. I do it in kindness. And if it be true that your shop cannot be supported without intoxicating drinks, as a friend, I advise you

---

17   1 Timothy 6:10, "For the love of money is the root of all evil: which while some coveted after, they have erred from the faith, and pierced themselves through with many sorrows."

to give it up, let the sacrifice be what it may; for better is it that yon sacrifice your money, than that you should, for the sake of money, sacrifice the welfare of your fellow-men." I would simply remark that if every professed temperance man would take the ground that my good employer did, *genteel grog* (wine, porter, ale, &c.) would be banished as a matter of policy from our fashionable confectioneries.

I must defer the remainder of my history to another number.

Yours, &c.

No. III.

ONE would suppose that, after all the sad lessons I had learned, I could now manage to keep out of the way of temptation, or that, if it obtruded itself on my path, I should certainly come off victorious. But no one knows the dangers that beset the reformed drunkard's path, or the need which he has of all the aid that can be obtained to enable him to hold on his course, but the reformed drunkard himself. Temptation assails him in every shape, in the midst of all his pursuits, trials, enjoyments, and sorrows, and with enticements addressed not only to his senses, but to his vanity, his desire of approbation, his reason even, and especially to his social feelings.

But to my story. On the way to and from my boarding-house, I had to pass by a family grocery where rum was sold, but sold rather secretly, at least out of sight of *front-shop customers*. It was a very neat and well-stocked shop on a corner, and the keeper of it, Mr. Acker, was a very pleasant, sociable, accommodating man—always ready to bid the passerby "good morning," and inquire kindly after his health, and that of his family. He was often at the door as I passed, and would sometimes so accost me that I could not help stop-ping to talk with him. And a social man, fond of conversation, on being invited politely to sit down in a chair which chanced to be close to the door could hardly refuse. The politeness of Mr. Acker, and the fact that I often saw there among his customers, not only the Rev. Mr. Clark (who liked such weddings, the reader will recollect, as they had in Cana of Galilee) but another clergyman who professed to be a strong temperance man, though he had never signed the total-abstinence pledge, and also some of the most consistent temperance men in the town, gradually lessened the abhorrence which I first had of a shop where J knew my chief enemy, Alcohol, bore rule. I accordingly often stopped in at a place where there was so much good company, and, as I was always a pretty good hand to tell a story, I was often flattered by the attention and applause of the little auditory which I sometimes found there. Behold me then again, gentle reader, a sort of oracle of a rum-shop,

not a dirty, low groggery,—but nevertheless a groggery—and with
parsons and deacons, and other very "honourable" and good men
for hearers;—not that they ever drank there, or saw others drink,
but they knew that rum was x only a few feet from them, kept from
their sight by a partition wall of an inch thickness.

I saw some strange scenes in that shop. A man once came in,
and asked Mr. Acker if he had some good hams. "First rate," said
Mr. A., and as he happened to be busy at the moment with another
customer, he asked him to go to the back-shop and pick one out of
the barrel for himself, the man went in, and soon came out eating
a cracker. "Well," said Mr. Acker, "didn't you find one to suit you
?" "I couldn't find them at all," said he. "You got the wrong barrel,
Sam, and found something else," said a queer-looking fellow, sitting
by. "I found a cracker," replied Sam, very gruffly. "But you generally wash crackers down with something, don't you?" said the other.
Mr. Acker did not like this joking, on account of some temperance
customers who stood in the door. So he cut the matter short by
gently pushing Sam through the door into the back shop, saying in
his complaisant way, "I will show you the hams, Mr. Mason." None
of them suited—they were all either too large or too small. The
truth is he had no idea of buying—he had helped himself to liquor
and that largely too. As he marched out of the shop, which he did
in a straight line, not stop-ping to lay three cents on the counter
(as he probably had not any in his pocket,) his friend Ned cried
out to him, " you had better come and look at the hams again, Mr.
Mason—looking is cheap, especially when you treat yourself into
the bargain." "That's a lie," said Sam, looking back fiercely, but still
moving off. "Come back and let us smell your breath," bawled Ned.
But he was off, for the subject was not agreeable to him, neither
was it to Mr. Acker, for he disliked to have his front-shop temperance customers know anything about the dram-drinking part of his
establishment.

One day I saw a man come into Mr. Acker's shop intoxicated.
His clothes were of fine texture, and were nearly new, but they had
evidently had some hard usage of late, I saw at once that he be-

longed to that class of drunkards who do up their drinking almost wholly in occasional sprees, the intervals between them being spent in tolerable, sobriety. He asked for rum. Mr. Acker refused him, telling him that he had drank too much already. "You gave me some the other day," said the man. "Well, you were not drunk then." "You knew I should be," said he, "you knew that I was on one of my sprees. Then was the time to deny me, if you wanted to do me any good. I don't believe you would deny me now, if Mr. Ames was not here," turning to a gentleman who was examining some very nice sugar. "You want to keep in with your cold-water customers." These were home truths, and the abashed rum-seller coloured, stammered, talked of impudence, and turned the man out of his shop.

After witnessing this scene I did not visit Mr. Acker's shop for some time, but his politeness and the example (mark that, reader, if you patronise such shops) the example of his wise and good patrons soon drew me in again. The back shop, all this time, I never entered, and supposed I never should. One day when I felt rather unwell, Mr. Acker offered me some "tonic bitters,: and very kindly fixed some for me in a glass. It made me feel rather better at the moment and I bought a bottle of it to take home. Wine bitters and hot drops, and sirups, into which is put "just brandy enough to keep them," as it is said, are dangerous things for the reformed drunkard to tamper with; and physicians and others should be very careful how they recommend them. My bottle of "tonic bitters" had enough of alcohol in it to wake up my old appetite in all its force, and when its contents were gone, I found my way into Mr. Acker's back-shop day after day, and was never refused by this respectable, polite, and very conscientious rum-seller till I became absolutely intoxicated. Then he turned me off, and I resorted to the worst grog-shop in town, and there gave myself up to drinking. It was the respectable Mr. Acker's rum, too, that I drank there, for the keeper of this groggery bought all his liquor of him. I staid there night after night, and for a week there was no moment that I was not drunk.

Who, think you, now sought me out, and plucked me from the fangs of the rum-seller? Not my employers. They felt for me, but they were discouraged, and gave me up for lost. They made no effort to get me away from this "suburb of hell,"—as Judge Daggett rightly calls the dram-shop. But Wilson, the generous-hearted sailor, who had been a sober man ever since I rescued him, now in turn rescued me. As soon as he heard of my downfall, he came to me, and amidst the sneers and gibes and the curses of the dram-seller and his crew led me away to my home.

What was now to be done? I could have no further hope of favour from my employers, and on the whole I concluded that a large town, where temptation meets the drunkard on every hand, was no place for me to hope for a lasting reformation. I therefore at once bid adieu to W—, and started off to seek out some farmer who had not a grog-shop within many miles of him, who would be willing to hire me as a labourer.

After some search I at length found a good old deacon, Mr. Alden, who chanced to want an additional labourer. I frankly told him my story, and my design in hiring myself out to him. He agreed to take me on trial. The farm was in a lovely spot, about three miles from the centre of the village of F—. In that centre were a church, two taverns and a grog-shop. Here, thought I, in this quiet nook, three miles away from rum, I shall be free from temptation and therefore secure from my besetting sin. But when I came to sit down to the tea-table my spirit sunk within me, for I found that the old serpent was here also. A tumbler was on the table here and there, and a pitcher of cider. The deacon drank two tumblers full, as he was uncommonly tired and thirsty. As I was aware of my danger, I refused to take any, and after tea I had a free conversation with the deacon on the dangerous example that he was setting before me. I saw that it was a trying case. He had drunk cider all his life time, and thought that it had always done him good, and therefore could not see it to be his duty to give it up. He allowed that, if it was true that it was dangerous for me to drink it, I had better not, for the present at least, but remarked that *by-and-by* it might be safe for me to drink *moderately*. He knew not then what a perilous doctrine he was preaching to a reformed man, but he found it out afterward.

A Reformed Drunkard

A man worked for him, one day, that got beastly drunk on some of his cider in default of rum, and then went home and turned his family out of doors, and beat his wife almost to death with a stick of wood. But even this did not convince the deacon of his error—so hard is it to remove confirmed habits or opinions. My case was destined, however, to reveal to him the truth on this subject. For a long time I abstained from drinking cider, although it was before me every day, and my appetite and the example of the good old man were arguments almost irresistible. At length in an evil moment I ventured to take *half* a tumbler, not a whole one. *It was only a little*—this was the flattering unction applied in this case as it was when I took the sip of wine. Next day I drank another half a tumbler and *a little more*, and the next day a full one. The deacon saw it, but did not warn me, for I drank so *little*, that he thought I was safe enough. At the end of a week, my appetite was thoroughly aroused, and as I chanced to be at work near the house after dinner, and the bunk door was open, I found my way to the barrel in the cellar several times in the afternoon. At supper time I was so drunk that I could neither walk nor talk straight! Deacon Alden was taken completely by surprise, and as he had become a good deal attached to me he felt very badly.

The next day we sat down under the big elm in his front yard and had a long talk together. I, a drunkard and a sinner, preached there total abstinence to a pious deacon, and, what is more, converted him. I descanted at length on the dangers which the customs of society place in the way of the reformed man, and, after giving him my views of the duties which the temperate owe to the drunkard, especially when he manifests a desire for reformation, I told him plainly that it was his example that was the occasion, of my present downfall, and I besought him, if he had any regard for the salvation of a fellow-man, to refrain from setting an example which it was not safe for me to follow. The appeal was not in vain. After hearing all that I had to say, he looked steadily on the ground and uttered his usual "Wal, wall" in his usual measured tone, and I knew something then was coming in the shape of a conclusion. I trembled lest it should be a wrong conclusion for me. "Wal, wal," said he, "Mather, my cider shall all be made into vinegar." I jumped up for joy. I felt like a freeman, escaped again from the toils of my enemy, and as I confidently hope, it was my final escape. At the dinner table deacon Alden gave his family a good tee-total lecture, and we voted the cider into perpetual banishment. Would that every farmer's family would do the same!

I have had no downfalls since I fell over the deacon's cider-barrel, more than two years since. Soon after my reformation at that time I became a religious man, and a little more than a year ago I married one of deacon Alden's daughters. I have a little boy a few weeks old, whom I have named after John Hawkins. My friend Wilson, who was with me in the alms-house at Norwich, is also here, and is about to marry another of the deacon's daughters. Come on, Mr. Hawkins, and attend the wedding, and we will show you as happy a cold water company as you ever saw.

Yours, &c.

Mother! Mother! cried she

No. IV.

I SAID in my last communication that in the centre of the village of F—there were two taverns and a grog-shop. One of the taverns is kept by a Mr. Branson, a vile, noisy, profane man, who made his two sons sots years ago, and at length has made himself so. He is a sort of village black-leg, and has always been the leader in horse-races, turkey shooting, matches, &c. The other tavern is kept by a Mr. Wightman, an easy sort of man, a slip-shod kind of character, who likes to idle away his time in a bar-room, hearing stale jests, old stories, and village gossip. He generally sits tipped back in his chair, with his greasy hat canted to one side, leaving just room enough to allow an occasional scratch of the head, when the thinking powers residing therein are called into action. To every item of news or gossip his usual reply is, "I want to know!"—which is uttered with an awkward nasal twang. Whenever he broaches, as he often does, the only argument that ever entered his head in favour of his business, viz., that he could not get his living if he gave it up, I have thought him at least sincere, for I could not see that he was fitted for any thing, either in mind or body, but that favourite accomplishment, the shaking of the toddy stick.

The grog-shop is kept by a Mr. Mason, what the world calls a very respectable man—a shrewd, bustling, money-getting, gentlemanly fellow. He is very popular with the rabble, and he has a good deal of influence with the better sort, even though they often talk of him as perfectly devoid of principle. I have heard a man that trades with him largely, say, that he had no doubt that he had done more harm than any other four men in the village. He used to sell rum in those by-gone times, when the shutters on the windows had painted on them Brandy, Rum, Gin. Those were worn out in the service years ago, and the new ones have no such old-fashioned words upon them. His business has gone on about as well without sign or advertisement—his shop still continues to be the chief rum-fountain for the village. He owns a great deal of land in different directions, most of which once belonged to some of his customers, but gradually came into his hands, by a process which I need not stop to I explain. Strange as it may seem, Mr. Mason has been for a long time selectman and justice of the peace. Many of the paupers that came under his charge were made paupers by rum, and that peace, of which he is the justice, is certainly very often disturbed by his customers. It has happened several times that he has sat in judgment upon the results of his own rum, and once the criminal, on hearing his sentence, said to him in the presence of a very large audience, "It was your rum that made me fight." This was rather awkward at least, but he forgot it when he counted up his gains that night, as he shut up his shop. It is gain, the world over, it is gain, that destroys all sense of shame in the rum-seller's bosom.

The effects of the rum-traffic are the same in this village that you find every where else. Much of the misery produced by intemperance is concealed from the eye of the mere observer. There is no record in this world that can give any adequate idea of its amount or variety. The Omniscient eye alone sees it— the eye that can look into every domestic circle, every secret place, nay more, into every bosom. There is misery untold, unseen, worse, tenfold worse, than all that meets the eye or ear.

It has sometimes seemed to me that the visible results of the traffic have been uncommonly bad in this little village. I find by inquiries of different persons, that in the last five years there have been one murder, three suicides, three deaths by delirium tremens, two by convulsions, two by drowning, all the results of rum. One of the cases of delirium tremens I witnessed. What a scene! It was in winter. The mother and her children were gathered about their scanty fire, shivering with cold. On a bed lay a man with a face swollen and of a purple hue—the clothes all in disorder, and here and there upon them blood which he had occasionally vomited. Two men stood near watching him. Soon he roused from his momentary quietness, and then it took all their strength to hold him. He saw devils coming to torment him, and he struggled violently to get away from them. "Let me go, let me go," he cried, trembling like a leaf, the perfect picture of terror. "Oh! oh! don't torment me —this is hell upon earth." And so he continued to cry out and struggle till he fell back in a convulsion and died. One circumstance was a little singular. Through the whole of his delirium he occasionally saw the rum-seller, Mr. Mason, among the devils, and entreated him not to set them upon him! Could an artist possibly hit upon a more just representation of the cruelty of rum-selling, than a rum-seller delivering up the poor drunkard to the hands of devils to be tormented?

It was only a week or two after this that I saw another scene of quite as dreadful a character. There lived in a small house, half a mile distant from us, a widow with a little girl, her daughter. Her husband died of disease induced by intemperance, before he had wasted all his estate. She was left at his death with what is called "a pretty little property." Her only son was then about twenty-one years of age. He ran a rapid career of dissipation, wasting still farther their rather scanty means, instead of making them a competence, as he might have very easily dope. He at length went to sea. His mother became disheartened, and instead of being improved in her character by her afflictions, she grew fretful and unhappy, and herself resorted to the battle for relief from her troubles. To her little daughter she was most ardently attached—her intemperance, gross as it was, did not destroy in her bosom all natural affection, as it sometimes does. And the little girl loved her in return as ardently. Loathsome and brutal as she often was in her drunkenness, still she, was her mother,—the only human being from whom she received any kindness day by day, the only one that took care of her and attended to her hourly wants. And if she sometimes abused her in a drunken fit, the fondness which she showed to her when she became sober would make the light-hearted little creature forget it all. After a while Mrs. Garner became miserably poor; her land, and even most of her furniture having passed gradually into the hands of the *respectable* Mr. Mason. She now sent out her little girl every day to beg. Every body felt an interest in little Mary Garner—in spite of her rags, there was something about her exceedingly attractive. Accordingly she always went home with a well-filled basket. Mrs. Garner managed to live along, as many such characters do, by what means one could hardly make out. It was a miserable life, but life it was. When it almost ceased to be life, as it sometimes did, the town would give its grudged pittance. AU this time, Mr. Mason, the selectman, who doled out the charities of the town, supplied her with rum, and not without pay, mark that, gentle reader. Rum is paid for often when nothing else is.

Early one morning as I passed by her house, I saw the door wide open, and something lying very near it against a high snow bank, which I found was Mrs. Garner. She was dead. Her clothes were much burnt, and so was her body. From the appearance of things I at once concluded that she had caught her clothes on fire, and had ran out, and had rolled herself in the snow to put out the flames, and then had lain down in a state of exhaustion and died. It was a bitter cold night, and she was frozen stiff. It was a horrid sight. I went into the house and there I saw a few smouldering embers in the fire-place, and near by stood a stand, on which was a candlestick, the candle having burnt down to the socket, a bottle with a little rum left in it, and a tumbler. In an adjoining room lay little Mary asleep, unconscious of the dire realities about her. I shut the door and went to call the neighbours. When we returned, the little girl had roused from her sleep, and finding that her mother was not there, had just opened the door and saw her lying dead. Such piteous cries I never heard. "Mother, mother, dear mother," cried she, wringing her hands. When she came to take hold of her cold hand she started back with* a shriek, and when she saw her crisped and blackened flesh, she fainted. When she roused, the first word she uttered was "mother," in a faint whisper, and she kept repeating it louder and louder as she revived, and for a long time she cried out, "mother, mother—do wake her—she is not dead— no, dear mother is not dead." It seemed difficult for her to realize that she was dead—the mother, who the night before had put her to bed, and kissed her and bade her good night so kindly—for this Mrs. Garner did before her solitary and fatal debauch.

It was necessary that the town should defray the expense of her burial, and for this purpose Mr. Mason called. I happened to be there when he came. As he entered, the little girl seemed to shudder and shrink away from him as from a viper, as worse than a viper he had been to her. I knew the cause, and I knew too that

59

the bottle which stood on that stand was filled the day before at his shop. I gave that man such a lecture as he never had before* He was ashamed, and angry, and conscience- stricken. But there was no penitence and no pity. His reply to it all was, "If I had not sold it to her, somebody else would." "Mr. Mason," said I, "dare you look on that blackened, stiffened corpse, and repeat what you have just said—*If I had not sold it to her, somebody else would! If I had not made this house desolate, and this little girl motherless, somebody else would! If I had not burnt up her mother, somebody else would! How does that sound, Mr. Mason?*" "I don't want any of your temperance lectures, Mr. Mather," said he, with a toss of the head. "If such a scene as this will not touch your heart," replied I, "no temperance lecture from me or any one else will reach it. But remember, there is a day of reckoning, when these horrid results of your business will confront you, and no sneer of yours can turn them aside. Your cold indifference will all be gone then." He muttered something about my minding my own business, and then proceeded to make the arrangements for the funeral in as unfeeling a manner as he had often done for other paupers.

In came also Mr. Wightman, from sheer curiosity. He sat down by an old crone who loved a drop now and then, and as she detailed to him the circumstances of the case, he would utter every now and then his usual stupid Response, "I want to know." He went straight home to his bar, as Mr. Mason did to his counter, to deal out as freely as ever—what shall I call it—"distilled death and darnation?"—a hard name, it is true, but who, in view of such a case, will not say it is a *just* one?

In my next I shall give an account of some instances of reformation among us, for we have been at work here in the temperance cause during the past year, and have met with the same encouraging results that have been so extensively realized in other places.

Yours, &c.

No. V.

I PROMISED in my last number to give in my next a description of some cases of reformation in our village. We have had some of a very interesting character, and a sketch of them will afford a key to some of the principles on which the present temperance movement is based, and must depend for its success.

The reader will recollect that I said there were two taverns in the centre of the village— one kept by a Mr. Wightman, a lazy, slipshod, inoffensive sort of a man, and the other by a Mr. Branson, a vile, noisy, profane gambler, but shrewd and active, and of pretty good appearance. His tavern was of course the popular one. In front of it is a piazza running its whole length, and a long bench is fastened against the wall between the two doors. Under this piazza you might often see on a summer's day quite a little collection of village worthies telling stories, or discussing politics, and other grave matters. Among them were some rather strongly marked characters. Reader, let me introduce you to them. That man with a weather-beaten face, of a frank, free-hearted expression, with a bold dash of the humorous, is Captain Carson, who has followed the seas his life. He is a jovial man, full of anecdote, and shrewd and sententious in his remarks. He is just now telling a story. See how his little audience swallow his yarn, with mouths wide open. Close by him sits a Mr. Clark, with his hat canted to one side, with an expression of countenance in which you can read his intention to beat the Captain's story as soon as he finishes it. He is a knowing man. He can talk theology with the parson, medicine with the doctor, law with the lawyer, in short, every thing, with every body, with perfect ease and assurance. Meanwhile he supports not his family, but they support him. Yet he walks about, flourishing his cane, which he does with a grace all his own, as if he was a man on whom not only a family, but the whole community depended. He is in the habit of telling large stories, especially when a little moved by the spirit within, and the Captain is always fond of quizzing him about Ins stories. Listen to him now. Captain Carson has just finished his story about a poor sailor, who suffered vastly from an inflamed foot, far away from land, the treatment of which he managed, of course, Successfully. "Well," says Mr. Clark, "now Captain, you didn't manage that foot right. It might have been Cured in less-than half that time. I once had an inflammation in my foot. I applied a poultice made with catnip, and wormwood, and Indian posy and rum (describing very minutely the mode of preparation and application,) and the result was that the inflammation all went into the great toe, and then when it went from there it popped like a pistol!"—giving a very graceful toss up of his cane—"Pon my word, it did." "Did it split your toe, and did it hit any body, Mr. Clark?" asked the Captain with the most quizzical look imaginable. But in spite of the ridiculousness of the story, and the burst of laughter which followed the Captain's inquiry, Mr. C. swore that it was true as gospel.

That bold-looking man that stands leaning against the pillar of the piazza, is Mr. James, a thoroughly bad man, the most intimate friend of Mr. Branson, and like him, a gambler. He has some wit— enough to make a joke against every thing good—sufficiently witty to excite a laugh among the frequenters of a tavern. Next to him stands a roughly dressed man, Mr. Johnson, who was once a farmer, and owned a very large farm, which he lost by rum and the law. The geese of a neighbouring farmer were very troublesome, and he shot several of them. They then went to law about this and some other matters, and were in a constant quarrel for many years keeping up their spunk all this time with rum—else they would have settled their difficulty almost at the outset. The conclusion was, that both lost their farms, and both became drunkards. Vastly more foolish were they than the geese they quarrelled about, and yet that Mr. Johnson, you can see by his face, is not naturally a fool. Rum often makes wiser men than he very foolish.

Now let me draw your attention to that grave-looking man that sits in an arm-chair opposite the captain. It is Squire Jones, a lawyer. He is seen in Mr. Branson's piazza only occasionally, and he is very cautious not to take his seat there except with company rather above the loafer order. You see a few of the ragged and dirty-shirted drinkers standing around. When they form any thing more than the out-skirts of the little company there assembled, he retires, though he is as much of a drunkard as any of them. He drinks mostly in private, and very seldom at a bar.

An amusing incident occurred some time since in relation to Squire Jones. At a temperance meeting Captain Carson was present, out Squire Jones was not, though many of his friends were and some of his immediate relatives. After the lecturer had finished his remarks, Captain Carson, who was rather tipsy, got up and said, " I spose, though I d—don't know, that I'm the only drunkard p—present in the s—sembly, but (raising his voice to a high pitch ana looking all around) Squire Jones wh—where are *you*—I say, Squire Jones, where are *you*?" The effect on the audience Jou can imagine better than I can describe, t was placing the secret, genteel, parlour-drunkard just where he belonged, on a level with the open, bar-room sot. "But Squire Jones where are you," became at once a byword in the village, and it is to this day at the tongues' ends of all the boys in the streets.

That short little man with a quick moving black eye, that stands behind the wise Mr. Clark's chair, is a Mr. Crowell, a shoemaker, and a first-rate one he is too. He is a periodical drinker for the most part. He loses enough of his time, and spends enough of his earnings, to make his family miserably poor; though, if it were not for this single habit, he would be as good a husband and father as there is in the village. He has long been the dupe of the vile Mr. Branson and his friend Mr. James, who continue to filch from him all his loose change whenever he gets on a spree. He is a social man, and you see he is enjoying the conversation to the full.

Now just notice for a moment that ragged, dirty, long-bearded man, that is hitching a horse to that post. It is Mr. Branson's hostler. He steps up into the piazza to join the group of drunkards, and dares to crack a joke even with the Squire, for he knows that the Squire loves brandy as well as he loves rum. How brutal he is in his whole appearance! He is gone by—you will say—there is no hope of nim. But that same man, reader, has been in the high places of the earth in point of privileges, and he was dragged down from thence by intemperance into the miry filth of the bar-room and the grog-shop. Is there no power to bring him back again ? Yes, blessed be God, there is.

So, I have introduced you, reader, to most of the characters in the group in Mr. Branson's piazza. Let me take you to the same spot again a few months after. The group you see is *smaller* now. Captain Carson is not there. Why? He is a reformed man, and the President of the Washington Total Abstinence Society, lately formed in our village, of which I have the honour to be Secretary. Mr. Crowell, the little shoemaker, is not there. He also is reformed, and his family are happy, and he is now at his last, working for their support, instead of idling away his time in gossip under Mr. Branson's piazza and drinking at nis bar. Mr. Johnson, the farmer, is not there. He has ceased to be so much of a goose as to frequent Mr. Branson's bar, and is thinking about joining our Society. The hostler is not there, neither is he on Mr. Branson's premises. His rags he has cast off—he is changed back from the brute to the man—and that countenance which a few months ago was the seat of the stupid leer of the sot is now beaming with virtue and intelligence. Dr. Newton (for this same ragged hostler was once a physician of great promise) is now labouring as a lecturer in the service of our Society, and he intends soon to establish himself again in the practice of his profession. His history is an interesting one, and at another time I will give it to you.

Even Squire Jones is not there. But it is not because he has reformed—he is as much a drunkard as ever. It is because it has become more disreputable since the formation of our Society to be seen lounging about a tavern.

But who do now compose the group in that piazza? A sorry company of dirty loafers, with the wise Mr. Clark for an oracle, and the vile Mr. James for his echo. Mr. Branson's " occupation" is nearly " gone," and it is the intention of our Washington Society that it shall be entirely so.

Now if we look carefully at the *characters* of the persons whom I have described, we shall see why it is that some of them are reformed, and not others. Reformation is not a haphazard business. This will be found to be true—that *character* has vastly more to do with the question of a drunkard's reformation than the degree to which the intemperate habit has reached. I use the word character in its widest sense, as including all that makes up the man.

Of that little group Mr. Clark is altogether too wise to learn any thing, especially to learn the simple lesson of teetotalism. He knows all about it. He knows how to promote the cause of temperance better than priests and priest- ridden men and women and reformed drunkards. He is a very Solomon. He never will "become a fool that he may be wise"—not he.

But why was not the Squire reformed?

Could he not, with all his acuteness, see that he is running a career, which, if persisted in, will ruin his respectability, his happiness, his soul? He may see this at times, and tremble at the prospect for the moment, but it is soon forgotten. He has created in himself, secretly for the most part, an appetite, which it needs influences from without to help him to over-come; but wrapped up in the dignity which his station throws around him, he shuts up the avenues, by which these influences can reach him. He is left therefore to fight *alone* with temptation. His resistance is almost as a matter of course weak and soon given over. If he were the frank, open, social drunkard that Captain Carson was, he might then, like him, have been reached and perhaps recovered.

Compare now the case of Crowell, the shoemaker, with that of Branson's boon companion, the gambling Mr. James. Mr. Crowell was the more confirmed drunkard of the two, so far as the degree of appetite is concerned. He was often fairly in the gutter, while it is very seldom that Mr. James has been seen absolutely drunk. But Mr. Crowell had in his sober moments honourable feelings, a sense of respectability, affection for his family—these and other motives which could be appealed to. He was vicious only in consequence of his intemperance; while the intemperance of Mr. James was rather the *product* than the cause of his other vicious propensities.

This in my view is a very important distinction, in estimating the probabilities of reformation in different case. It teaches us one very useful lesson. *Never despair of the reformation, of any drunkard, however low he may have got in his intemperance—however strongly the disease, for it is such, is fastened upon him,* PROVIDED THAT WHEN HE IS SOBER, THERE ARE ANY GENEROUS FEEL-INGS IN HIS BOSOM, ANY GOOD MOTIVES, TO WHICH YOU CAN APPEAL WITH ANY SORT OF EFFECT. If there be one chord that you can touch and awaken proper feeling, per-severe in your efforts, though he fall again and again. But if the drunkard be a disorganizer, a hater of good doings, a bad citizen, a bad husband, and father *aside from intemperance*—if his heart be exceedingly depraved, and his drunkenness is merely a consequence of his badness of heart; there is no hope of his restoration, till his heart is changed—till the *source* of his intemperance and his other bad propensities is purged by religion. And this leads me to say that after all, *religion* must be made the *basis* of this temperance reforma-tion now going on, if we wish it to be thoroughly and permanently successful. Motives from other sources may be and often are ap-pealed to with great effect, such as regard for character, affection for one's family, self-respect and the desire for respectability, the love for rational happiness, &c., but still let it be written as with a sunbeam that the "rock of salvation" is the same to the drunkard as to every other sinner, the only *sure* rock of safety on which his feet can be planted.

In this connexion I notice a very interesting fact, that the ref-ormation of the drunkard is, in these days of wonders, often, very often, the means of introducing religion to his heart. How can it be otherwise? The man has been suddenly aroused from his delu-sive dream of vice. It seems to him, now that he has escaped from the spell with which the monster intemperance has so long bound him, that he has awakened to an entirely new world of thought and feeling. His bosom is accordingly opened to the influence of motives, and what motives are more calculated to act strongly upon him than those offered by religion? His heart too is softened by the kindness and sympathy, which have been extended to him by those who have prayed and laboured for his restoration. And as he looks back upon the degradation and misery from which he has been saved, how can he help breaking forth in thanksgiving to God, and devoting, with the deepest penitence and the warmest love, his future life to his service. I should like to dwell longer on this topic, but my limits warn me to close. I would merely add, let clergymen and all good men see to it, that they neglect not the wide field of usefulness laid open before them by the present temperance movement. Enter into it and reap the rich harvest.

In my next I will continue my sketches of the reformation in our village.

Yours, &c.

The Visit to Mr Crokers

No. VI.

THE Washington Society, though it has been in existence but a few months, has produced a very marked change in the aspect of our village. Lounging about the taverns, which has been an extensive business here, is now pretty much given up. Beside those who are fully reformed, there are many others who have of late kept away from the tavern, and many others still who do not go there so often as they used to do. The other day, as Mr. Wightman stood in his vacant bar-room, with his hands in his pockets, as usual, whistling, and looking out at the window, he saw his fellow tavern-keeper standing in his piazza, casting occasionally a wishful look up and down the street, probably to spy some old customer wending his way to the wonted point of attraction, but in vain. Sympathy prompted him to step across the way, and mingle his- sorrows with those of Mr. Branson. "Well, Mr. Wightman" said Mr. B., as he approached, "they say old Jim Jackson has joined the cold water fanatics." "I want to know!" drawled out Mr. Wightman, with the most lugubrious look imaginable. "These men are injuring our business, Mr. Branson,—they certainly are. Jest look. Why it's as melancholy as Sunday here in your piazza, and its jest so in my barroom." "Poh, poh, they'll all be back again, after the breeze is a little blown over." "You think so?" "Yes I do. There's Crowel got to drinking again, last training. To be sure, they say he made his confession, and promised not to drink any more. But he wont stick, you see if he does. And there's Johnson—he's been talking about joining; but he was at my house last night, and drank considerable, and so was Robinson, too." At this piece of comforting intelligence, Mr. Wightman's lugubrious countenance assumed an unwonted brightness, the lazy shrug of the shoulders was gone, he took his right hand from the pocket, to express his pleasure by a significant snap of the fingers, and uttered his usual, "I want to know," with vastly less of a drawl than he commonly did. What a miserable business rum-selling is, when those who follow it are driven to get their crumbs of comfort from the downfall of the reformed, and their return to degradation and woe!

Just at this moment, old Jim Jackson, as Mr. Branson called him, came along. He was an old man of sixty years, but appeared as if he were over seventy, for intemperance had made sad havoc of his physical energies. He was pale, and bent over, and tottering in his walk. What a wonder is this man's reformation! A habit of forty-five years' growth, adhered to in spite of all the evil which he saw it bringing upon him and upon his family, is as it were in a twinkling dislodged and cast out! An appetite which has grown with his growth and strengthened with his strength through a long life, and has thus bec6me a part of the man, is in his old age resisted and conquered! What a victory! Well may we call such cases a resurrection. Men, dead for years, (some, like this man, for nearly half a century) to all the motives of interest, and affection, and reason, have arisen like men, to act like men! Men, doomed, as it appeared, to death, and that the hopeless death of the drunkard—anticipating the horrors of that death by self-inflicted misery and woe—living year after year just this side of absolute death, and all the time in danger of death from the thousand accidents to which the drunkard is exposed—given up by their friends and the community, not only as outcasts, but as lost, and in that sense dead—is it not like a resurrection, to see such men arise, and cast off their rags, and purge themselves of their filth, and stand up in the face of day, and speak out like men "the words of truth and soberness," and ring their loud appeals in the ear of the cruel murderers of their peace, the rum-sellers!

"Well, Mr. Jackson," said Mr. Branson, so you have joined the cold water society." "Yes, I have; have you any objection sir?" "Why, I don't see how so old a man can break right off. You'll get sick I'm afraid," said Mr. B., with an awkwardly-assumed tone of kindness.

"Your vile stuff has kept me sick for years back, all the time. I believe that if I had never drank any of it I should be as straight and nimble as any other man of sixty." "But I thought," said Mr. B., "that it was the rheumatism that bent you over so." "A great deal of what people call rheumatism ought to be called *ru*matism," quickly replied Mr. Jackson. The old man then went on to give these two drunkard-makers quite a lecture of a very practical character, and Mr. Branson was rather sorry that he stopped him to talk with him, just as many other rum-sellers have been sorry when they have drawn a reformed man into a discussion. It is a kind of contest in which they are pretty apt to get beaten. A reformed man, speaking of the blessedness of the change from drunkenness to sobriety, is such a living demonstration of the baseness of their business, that they quail under his well-directed shafts.

A few days ago I chanced to be passing the old man's house. Every thing about it looked very differently from what it did a few weeks ago. No hats and rags were stuffed out of the windows—the broken gate was mended— the rubbish strown about the yard was all gathered up—in short, a different genius seemed to preside Over the whole scene. "Windows all mended up, Mr. Jackson," was my salutation. "Yes, a pane of glass costs only just as much as a glass of grog," was the characteristic reply. I could not help going in to see whether the reform was as great inside as it was outside. I found it Jo be still more complete, just as I expected. For home, the place where the reformed drunkard finds his chief delight when he has such a wife as Mrs. Jackson is, is the place where of all others the reform is most manifest. The change is thorough here. The vestiges of intemperance are effaced most effectually of all from the fireside. The contrast between former penury and misery, and Cresent thrift and happiness, is most observable ere. The wife, rejoicing over her husband's reform, with alacrity plies her every art, to make this spot all that home should be. Perhaps through her discouragements she had in years past become somewhat of a slattern; out now a load seems taken from her, and with light foot she springs about, and manages to keep the whole house in perfect order and cleanliness. The windows let in a bright light, unobstructed by dirt and cob-webs, upon the scoured tables and floors, and the shining tins and dishes, and the whole aspect of things is cheerful.

It was thus that I found matters at old Mr. Jackson's. His wife is a quick-moving, black-eyed little woman, who has, in spite of her husband's drunkenness, accomplished a good deal in her day. She has brought up a large family of children, who are all well settled in the world. Two of her children, a son and a daughter, were at home at this time on a visit. They wept tears of joy, as the good old woman blessed me as the chief instrument of her husband's reformation. I wept, too, reader, for I could not help it. And I often weep, as I think of myself, once the degraded, ragged, miserable inmate of the Alms-House at Norwich, and now taken out of the very mire of intemperance, and exalted to be a co-worker with God himself in redeeming others from the same degradation! Why is it that I, instead of having been, like thousands of others, chased out of this world by the scorpion stings of delirium tremens and made to fill a drunkard's grave, and go down to a drunkard's doom, have been thus plucked as a brand from the burning, and even been honoured as an instrument of salvation to others? The grace of God, *the grace of God*, has done it.[18]

A little distance beyond Mr. Jackson's, stands the house of a Mr. Crocker, at which I called the same day. Here I found a very different scene. The fences were broken down, the fate was bolstered up with a log, the yard was umbered up with all sorts of broken things, an axe lay across some rails (probably stolen) which were partly cut up for firewood. I opened the door, which hung rather dubiously at least upon its hinges, and went in. The windows were stuffed with hats and coats, and the panes that were still in, were covered with dust and cobwebs, casting 'a dim,' but not 'religious light,' into as gloomy and disordered an apartment as you ever saw. A table stood in the middle of the room, with fish-bones, pota-to-skins, slops, dirty crockery &c., scattered over its greasy surface. Two ragged boys stood by the scanty fire. On a bed lay a sick child, its pale face peeping out from under a pile of ragged bed-clothes. In a chair was tied a little chubby fellow, crying with all his might because its patience was wearied out. The sluttish mother, who was busy washing dishes as I came in, cried out to the little one with a horridly harsh voice, "be still," and as that did not answer, she twitched it out of the chair and gave it a good shaking, and then as it cried louder still, she picked up a piece of bread from off the dirty floor, and putting it into the child's hand, said "there, take that and

18   Big Book, p.25, "But for the grace of God, there would have been thousands more convincing demonstrations."

see if you can't stop your noise." To cap the climax, at one end of the room sat Crocker himself, with patched, filthy clothes, his beard of a week'§ growth, his hat dented in upon one side and pulled over his eyes, tipped back in his chair in a drunken sleep. A shake not of the gentlest kind from his spouse produced a grunt—another made her lord, in attempting to scratch his head and yawn, knock his hat off, and then, "here, Mr. Crocker, Mr. Mather wants to see you," uttered in the harshest tone ever woman's voice put on, roused this piece of flesh to motion. He saluted me with a how d'ye do and a nod, not exactly in Chesterfieldian style.

After I had done my errand, I talked with him about drinking. He said that he did drink but little. "Noone," said he, "can say that they ever saw me drunk. I've been a little elevated I know training days and so on, but—no, not drunk, Mr. Mather—no, not drunk, sir." As he said this, he cast a sideway glance at his hat, as if he wanted to pick it up, but hardly dared to venture the attempt lest he should show that he was even then rather more than "a little elevated." "If you don't drink but little," said, "how is it that you are so poor?" "I have a great family to support, I would have you know, sir," replied he, straightening himself up with great dignity. "Yes, yes," added his wife, who also loves the bottle poor folks, Mr. Mather, have to get along as they can." "I know," said I, "that you have a large family, but if you drink no rum yon might have enough, and you and your children need not be ragged as you now are." "You seem to despise my clothes, sir, and I know they are none of the best. But I am a working man, sir, and dress accordingly, sir. I cares very little for outside show, sir. I go for comfort here, sir," putting his hand to the region of his heart. I thought he meant the comfort of the good creature, as he was wont to *go* for that kind of comfort pretty often to the tavern and rum-shop. But he added, as explanatory, "a good conscience is the thing, sir. I go for that, and not for outside show, sir." Such was the laughable reply of this ragged, filthy wretch, covered all over and surrounded on all sides with the "outside show," of drunken poverty. The conversation continued for some time longer, and this conscientious despiser of "outside show," prated of the dangers with which cold-water societies threaten the liberties of the country. What great patriots, what sentinels on the watch towers of liberty, drunkards are, yes, and rum-sellers too!

If my limits would permit, I would describe one or two more interesting cases of reformation in our village, contrasting them with cases of an opposite character, but I must close. Our Washington Society is in a flourishing condition. We meet together very often, and once in a while we have a public meeting in the meeting house. We have a curious mixture of the grave and the comical at some* of our meetings of a familiar character which we hold at different houses in the village. Our president, Capt. Carson, and Wilson, the generous sailor, who was with me in the almshouse at Norwich, amuse us with their "yarns." Dr. Newton, the quondam hostler of Mr. Branson, is always full of instruction, and the other members detail a great variety of facts, and make many very shrewd remarks, I will give you a description of one of our public meetings in my next.

Yours, &c.

A Reformed Drunkard

No. VII.

IN this number I will fulfil the promise, made in my last, to give a description of one of our temperance meetings.

I shall not attempt to give a full report of the different speeches, but shall make such extracts from them as I think will interest the reader. The first speech was made by Captain Carson, which was well-spiced with nautical phrases. After describing some incidents from nis own personal experience to illustrate the evils of intemperance, he thus concluded: "So, you see, my friends, that all my life time I have been running on shoals and quicksands and rocks. You know how it is with the rum-sellers—they are all along every coast, holding out false lights to decoy the mariner on the sea of life, and when they have made him run on the rocks, and he is wrecked, they have no pity for him—not they. They busy themselves in picking up all of the wreck they can lay their hands on, and they leave the poor manner to take care of himself—and if he perish, they care not—O, these wreckers can't leave their *profitable and honourable* business just then to throw him a bit of rope, or reach him a hand, or heave him a plank. A box of goods, or a piece of the wreck is more *profitable* to them, than the salvation of a sailor's life or his soul—and so, if they are side by side, they'll haul up the box, or the piece of wreck, and let the sailor sink to a watery grave!

This is not all. There is a set of men, commonly known as Washingtonians, that are here and there along *some* coasts, who are always on the lookout for the shipwrecked mariner. They have their life-boats, and they are ever ready to throw a rope, or to do any thing to save their fellow-men from destruction. But I have known these wreckers to destroy their life-boats, and even to take away from the Washingtonians their planks and ropes, and that too, when the cry for help was ringing in their ears. I'll tell you what I saw once with my own eyes. A poor sailor, was swimming to the shore, and, exhausted with the effort, was just ready to sink. A Washingtonian threw out to him a rope, and as he held one end in his hand, one of these wreckers attacked him, and undertook to take from him the rope. The struggle was a severe one; but, thanks to God, the Washingtonian *held fast to the rope*, and threw the rum-seller off with all his might—and then, heave O, and the sailor was saved. O, what joy filled the sailor's heart; yes, and the good Washingtonian's too! That sailor, my friends, was the speaker—and what reason have I to bless the Washingtonians, and I was going to say, to curse these wreckers, the rum-sellers. But no. Hard and cruel as their treatments of me has been, I must not curse or hate them—rather, I must pray for them, that they may repent, and cease to do this great evil.

"But even this is not all. To cap the climax, these wreckers have the impudence to claim that their business is an honourable and honest business, and they raise a hue and cry about the Washingtonians, and complain that they are destroying their means of getting a livelihood ! O, it makes my blood boil to near them talk in this way, and it's hard work, I can tell you, to cool down enough to be able to pray for them.

"It's about time that my 'yarn' should stop. My life, till quite lately, has been, as you see, a tempest-tost kind of life. I have shipped many a heavy sea, and once in a while have been raked fore and aft. I've been capsized a good many times, especially when, being a little top-heavy, with not enough ballast, and under too much sail, I've run before the wind. Well, at length, I got to be a weather-beaten, dismantled, worn-out hulk. But, my friends, the old ship is not *unseaworthy* yet. She's lately got new masts, and new rigging, and is painted up bright, and she'll mind her helm a good deal better than she used to do. O what a crooked course I have run. I've been beating *about* all my life time, but now I've got on the right tack, and I am going a straight course, with a fair wind, and sail all set, and I EXPECT TO MAKE A GOOD HARBOUR."

The next speaker was Mr. Crowell, the shoe-maker. After making some interesting remarks on the contrast between his former miserable situation as a drunkard, and his pre-, sent happiness as a reformed man, he went on to say—"Let us cipher a little, my friends, on this subject, and see how the matter comes out in dollars and cents. If a man drinks a glass of rum a day, it amounts in a year, at 3 cents a glass, to 11 dollars—if two glasses, to 52 dollars. This is a pretty moderate allowance for a drinking man, however. Well, a man treats his friends once in a while, if he has any generosity. This will cost him at least 10 or 15 dollars a year—say 10. Add this to the 22 dollars, and it makes 32. Then too, a drunkard is very apt to get cheated, and I may say robbed too. Somehow his money will disappear wonderfully in a grog-shop or a tavern—faster a good deal than he can drink it up any how. It takes to itself wings and flies away, and I rather think they are *five-fingered wings* too. How much snail we add for this? Twenty dollars a year? That's quite little enough, according to my experience. This makes the whole 52 dollars in a year lost by drinking rum at the very lowest calculation you can put it.

"But this is nothing compared with the loss of *time* which drinking occasions. There's many a drunkard that loses almost all his time so far as his family is concerned—they have to support themselves, while he spends all he earns for rum. But we will suppose he loses two days in a week, which is quite a small calculation for a man that makes anything of a business of drinking. I've lost more than that for years back. Well, two days a week makes 104 days in a year, which at a dollar a day is worth 104 dollars, and most men can earn more than that. Add this to the 52 dollars already reckoned, and it makes 156 dollars. Now, if a man loses this every year for ten years, if we say. Nothing about interest, he loses 1560 dollars—enough to buy a comfortable house, and furnish it too.

"Now here it is in black and white. Figures don't lie. Why, if any thing, I havn't told the story bad enough. There are several farms in this town, worth a good deal more than 1560 dollars, that have been got rid of, some of them in less than ten years, by rum. And one fact must not be forgotten—some of these farms have got into the hands of the rum-sellers that sold their owners the rum which ruined them. Here let me tell you a short story of a farmer that once lived in a town near us. Fifteen years ago I knew him as a rich man, and I recollect going to his house at that time. I remember just how the furniture looked, and particularly a large family clock, which stood in the corner of the room, which was said to have cost 140 dollars. A few days ago I was in that town, and called on business at the house of a rum-seller. There I saw about the room some of this same farmer's furniture and in the corner stood that same old clock. I need hardly tell you the reason of this change. The farmer had died a drunkard, and his property, even to his furniture, had passed into the rum-seller's hands, *as the wages that his master, Satan, had given him for ruining that man.*"

Mr. Crowell was followed by Dr. Newton. "That story about the old clock," said he, "what a lesson on the sad changes produced by intemperance! What a lesson, too, on the responsibilities of the rum-seller, and the dread account he must at last render of the wide-cast evil he has done in this world! There that clock stands in that rum-seller's house with its solemnly slow but steady tick, tick, tick, day and night, while its rightful owner sleeps in the silence of the grave—and that too, a drunkard's grave! O, if that rum-seller would only think, as he hears that old servant thus speak, how many swiftly flowing years it kept the reckoning of time for a happy family, and how many wearisome years it kept the same reckoning for the same family in their misery, and that misery occasioned by *him*—how many nights the pale, care-worn wife sat listening to its lonely sound even to midnight, waiting for her husband's return, while he was carousing in *his* shop—and if he would think, as he now hears that ever-recurring tick, tick, tick, that every swing of that pendulum brings him one moment nearer to the time, when he must meet his victim face to face in judgment —when time shall be no longer, and retribution, measured by no reckoning of time, shall begin never to end. Ah, if he would think of all this, how would he be overwhelmed with the extent of the ruin he had produced—ruin that shall abide after that clock shall cease to tell of time, after these busy scenes of earth are passed away, after the world itself is burned up—yea, *for ever*—**FOR EVER**. But no— that rum-seller does not think of all this—he puts down his conscience, which ever and anon rises like a ghost to upbraid him—he shuts out from his sight, so far as he can do it, the horrid results of his traffic in this life, and looks not beyond to another—he goes on heaping up his pile of shining dust, reckless of the misery he is scattering about him. But the time will soon come, when his hand shall relax its grasp on the 'muck rake,' with which he scrapes up that perishable pile—when the visions of earth shall become dim to his sight—when the ticking of that clock shall grow fainter and fainter upon his ear—he dies—and after death the judgment—and what after that! Ah, the clock of eternity will strike upon his ear, slow and heavy, tick—tick—tick—never to run down, but to go on, tick—tick—tick—through the never-ending ages of his torment."

The impressive tone and manner with which this short address was delivered (whatever difference of opinion there might be in regard to it as a matter of taste) produced a breath- less stillness, which remained after the speaker was seated, like a spell which no one seemed to be willing to be the first to break. A little rustling, however, after a few moments began somewhere, which soon became quite general, and then, Captain Carson called upon my friend Wilson to address the meeting.

"The rum-seller" said he, "is pretty much the same thing the world over. I have encountered him in all shapes. It's a *cruel* business, and the man that follows it must either become a cruel man, or give it up. You have probably heard of the land-sharks in our cities that entice the poor sailors into their dens. I have often been stripped by them. I once had sixty dollars clear when I was paid off, and I was persuaded by one of these men to go to his boarding-house. In some way my money was all gone in a week—it all went into the pocket of that man—not that I drank so much —it was stolen. He stole away my senses with rum, and then he stole my money. And just so I have been served by rum-sellers every where. They all *steal*, whether they actually put their hands into the pocket or not. When they take the poor deluded drunkard's money, they give him nothing for it, or rather they give him worse than nothing—*poison*. The rum-seller that owns the farm of a drunkard, which has fallen into his hands through the rum that he has sold him, has *stolen* that farm. Many a house is built with money *stolen* from drunkards. But the rum-seller steals more than money and houses and farms from the poor drunkard—he *steals* his health, his happiness, his character—every thing that is valuable in this life or the life to come. In short, he steals the drunkard's money, his body and his soul—his money he keeps—his body he delivers over to disease—and his soul to his master, the devil."

Mr. Mason, whom the reader will recollect as the standing justice in our village, happened to be just finishing off a fine house, and he took fire at the remarks of Wilson. Pale and trembling he arose, and interrupted him. "I like temperance, Mr. Chairman," said he, "but some are intemperate in their temperance. They denounce too much, and call hard names. I have been called a thief here to-night I am not conscious of stealing from any one. I can lay my hand on my heart, and before this assembly and my Maker, assert that I am an honest man. If men buy rum of me it's an honest trade—they are the judges whether they get their money's worth or not. My maxim is, that if I sell to men of discretion, they know what use to make of what they buy, and I am not responsible for their abuse of it. No one can say that I ever sell to any one that has already drank too much."

When he said this there was a general murmur—it was evident that the truth of this statement was at least doubted, and Mr. Mason, it was plain had better have kept still. When Wilson replied to him, he exercised a commendable forbearance towards him; for he could have given the lie to his assertion with facts, but he contented himself with combating the *principles* advanced by Mr. Mason. He showed that the rum-seller is responsible for the bad use which "men of discretion," as Mr. Mason called them, make of the rum he sells them. "Take a common case," said he, "here is a man who is at first a moderate drinker. He drinks more and more from year to year till at length he becomes a drunkard. All this time the rum-seller, who supplies him with his rum, sees the gradual increase of the amount he buys, and sees too that just in proportion to that increase, poverty and wretchedness are coming upon him and his family. Is he not responsible for furnishing him with the means of this self-destruction, as really as if he put a dirk or pistol into his hands, knowing that he would with it commit suicide? And when the poor man has become a drunkard, and the rum seller has got out of him pretty much all that he can get, is it any credit to that rum-seller to refuse him any more rum? As well might the murderer claim credit for not *mangling* his victim after he had killed him.

"Let not the rum-seller say that he does not see that he is doing all this harm. If he have the common perceptions of a man, he does see it. Some of the rum-sellers are shrewd men—shrewd enough to make money fast at any rate, and if they don't see the harm they are doing they have a blindness on this point which they don't have on others. Mr. Mason is offended because I said the rum-seller *steals* from the drunkard, and says that he is not conscious of stealing from any one. All that I have to say about it is this—if he has not taken from the drunkard his property, and given him in return penury, misery and disease, he is different from all other rum-sellers. He calls the traffic in rum an honest trade. Is it honest to take men's money, and not only not give them an equivalent, but administer to them poison—a poison for body and soul. He talks of 'men of discretion.' Does the drunkard, spellbound by his appetite, sacrificing property, health, happiness—every thing to its gratification, act like a 'man of discretion?' And can the man who in cool blood ministers to his appetite for the sake of gain, find an excuse for his cruelty in his victim's 'discretion?' As well might he excuse himself for giving the suicide or murderers weapon, with the plea that that suicide or murderer is a 'man of discretion.'"

In my next, reader, I will give you the history of Dr. Newton, whom I introduced to you in my fifth number as Mr. Branson's hostler.

Yours, &c.

The death of Dr Newtons mother

No. VIII.

IN this number I will fulfil my promise to give the history of
Dr. Newton, who, the reader will recollect, was only a few weeks
ago the ragged dirty hostler of the vile Mr. Branson. The particulars
were communicated to me partly by himself and partly by his sister.

I shall begin with the period of his entering college. At that
time he was "the only son of his mother, and she a widow." She had
drank deeply of the cup of affliction, and she was literally "acquainted with grief." One after another of her family had died, till a large
circle had dwindled down to three; herself, this son, and daughter.
He entered Yale College at the age of fifteen. He was a lad of gentle
and winning manners, generous and noble in his disposition, enter-
taining as a companion, and therefore exceedingly popular among
all his associates. As he was confiding and unsuspecting he was an
easy victim of temptation. His social qualities introduced him at
once to a large circle of acquaintants, who caressed and flattered
him, and he soon became the dupe of a set of dissipated young
men in the upper classes who gave him frequent invitations to their
convivial meetings.

To the temptations thus presented by social enjoyment was
added the enchantment of poetry and music. Young Newton was
the finest singer in college, and of course, he soon learned the
Bacchanalian songs, which have so much disgraced the harp of
many a sweet poet; and no wonder that as he sung the praises of the
wine cup, and called it the "cup of kindness," and connected with
it all the delightful associations of "auld lang syne," he should drink
deeply of that cup, especially when he knew that it was not only the
theme of the poet, but was approved by the sage, and even blessed
by him that ministered at the altar, as the acknowledged symbol of
plighted friendship and love. He did not dream that he was then
really singing the song of the drunkard in the beginning of the high
road to ruin; much less that he would, after a few years had rolled
away, be found standing up as a redeemed man, among redeemed
men, singing the same notes to the joyful songs of the reformed.

He did drink deeply. The temptation of the wine cup often overpowered him, and he was soon fairly within the circling current of the whirlpool of drunkenness. Still, his ambition to excel, his fondness for literary pursuits, and the influences of the good, kept him for a long time from becoming confirmed in dissipation. It was true, he often "got high," but so did many of those who were called "steady fellows," and who held high rank as scholars, and some occasionally, who were members of the church, and that too without any very special notice being taken of it This appears strange to us, in these better times of light, but it was one of the sad results of the universal prevalence of the custom of wine drinking, for it was at that time universal in all the colleges in our country. It was even sanctioned by the officers of the college in the annual meetings of some of the literary societies at which they were present We do rejoice that it is not so now, and that the principles so well developed in the late sermon of Professor Ware now bear sway so extensively in the colleges of our land.

The standing of young Newton as a scholar, the two first years was, notwithstanding his habits, very high; but at length, his dissipation interfered so much with his studies that ne lost his rank, and though he would occasionally rise to it again, he easily relapsed, and he finally gave up all desire to do any thing more as a scholar, than what was absolutely necessary to secure him bis degree. Yet he was not in those times of wine-drinking called a drunkard.—He was "a high fellow" and liked a "spree[19]"—this was the language in which he was spoken of.

His mother and sister were borne down with sorrow and chagrin by his sad career. Still they hoped that as the bouyancy of youth passed away, and as he mingled in the practical realities of life's busy scene, he would "sober down" and become a "steady man." He hoped so too. He had no idea of becoming a drunkard. The very suggestion of such an idea prompted at once the feeling which Hazael had, when he exclaimed, "is thy servant a dog that he

19   Big Book, p. 21 "He uses his gifts to build up a bright outlook for his family and himself, and then pulls the structure down on his head by a senseless series of sprees."

should do this thing!" His sister undertook to talk with him serious-ly on this subject, when he was about to leave home to enter upon the study of medicine. "Poh, poh, Maria," was his reply, "you need not have any anxiety about me. I have sowed all my wild oats, and I'm going to make as wise and grave-looking a doctor now as you ever saw." It was thus lightly he spoke of his intemperance. Little did he think then that the spell was actually upon him, that was destined to become stronger and stronger, and at last, to draw him down into the lowest depths of drunkenness. He really did suppose that he had sowed all his wild oats, as he expressed it, and he en-tered upon the study of his profession with great zeal and assiduity.

But the wine cup was every now and then presented to him by the hand of friendship, and the vow of total abstinence he had nev-er breathed, and to its pledge he had never put his hand. A renewal of the same scenes that he passed through in college was the conse-quence. Still, after every season of dissipation, he aroused himself to study more easily than he did in college, because his studies now had a more immediate and palpable bearing upon the active duties of life. And as he had a strong native taste for the acquisition of knowledge, he readily acquired a very thorough medical education in spite of the drawbacks occasioned by his habits of dissipation. The letters, too, of that faithful sister, had a great effect upon him. Though he called her methodistical, and laughed about her fears that he would become a drunkard; yet, when he would say, "she's a lovely little saint, and I guess I had better mind her," though he said it in sport, he did often "mind her," and in doing so was held back from absolute ruin. But I must not dwell on this part of his history. Suffice it to say, that when he took his medical degree, the appetite for strong drink was more firmly fastened upon him, than it was when he left college. He was not, however, in his own view, nor in the view of his friends and acquaintances, a drunkard. But his sister, who, with the love of an *only* sister, watched his every movement, was fully aware of his danger, and continued to utter in his ears the notes of warning.

On taking his degree he went home to spend a few weeks

preparatory to his beginning practice. His mother was sick at the time and died soon after his return. On her death-bed she warned him faithfully, and when she besought him never to touch again the intoxicating-bowl, he made the vow on bended knees at her bed-side, and as he made it, with uplifted hand, his mother said, God help you to keep that vow, and his sister added, Amen. A few evenings after his walk with that sister he entered the burial-ground, and there over the grave of that sainted mother, she told him that though he had made that solemn vow, she was afraid when he came to mingle in the world he would yield again to temptation. "Why, do you think me so weak, Maria? You wrong me by uttering such a fear," said he. "Ah, brother, if you only felt your weakness, I should feel more safe about you. You feel strong and secure, just as you did, three years ago when you entered on your medical studies—you laughed at my anxiety then, and said that you had done with dissipation—but, you know how it has been with you since." "Well, well," said he impatiently, "I know, sister, that I've been a little wild, but now that I am going to settle down in actual practice, and shall see less of young men, I shall certainly be a steady, sober man. I have determined on eminence in my profession, and with this object ever before me I shall turn my back on frolicking and drinking. You look up at me as if you did not believe me. I feel hurt, Maria, I really feel hurt that you distrust me so." "I don't doubt your sincerity, William, in the least, but I do distrust your self-confidence. You talk of aiming at eminence in your profession, as if that would be a sure preservative from vice; but, brother, think how many *giants* in the career of ambition have been thrown down and even destroyed by the temptation of the wine cup. You have no such fear of the power of temptation as you ought to have, and you evidently place no reliance on divine aid—else you would have joined me in saying amen when our dear mother asked God to help you keep your vow. Depend upon it, William, if you wish to be safe, you must come to this humiliating point, for humiliating it is, I know, to the proud spirit of a young man. Temptation *will* overcome you again unless you meet it with a different spirit from what you have done." Truth, uttered in such tones of tenderness by an only sister over the grave of a beloved and faithful mother, at whose bed-side he had so recently made that solemn vow, melted him down. "I know it—I know it all, Maria," said he. "I have been proud and self-confident and thoughtless. God has not been in all my thoughts. I have not asked him to help me resist temptation. But this hour I trust that I shall never forget. Henceforth let other motives, and views, and feelings govern me. And, sister, you, I know, will never cease to pray for me." "Never—no, never—day and night for years you, my only brother, have been the subject of my prayers, and you will continue to be so. O, if I could see you cast away *for ever* the cup of intoxication, and come to the fountain of living water—how happy, how happy I should be!"

Who would think it possible that the hallowed influences of that hour could have resulted in any thing short of devotion to the service of God—much more that they could have been effaced, destroyed! But the magic witchery of the intoxicating bowl—what has it not destroyed on this fair and lovely earth! What so good as to be beyond the reach of its desolating blight!

Yours, &c.

The Visit to the Alms House.

No. IX.

DR. NEWTON (the remainder of whose history I will give in this number) opened an office in the large and beautiful town of S—. There was much gay society there, and, as the old pledge was then in vogue, the grave as well as the gay were in the habit of drinking wine at parties, and especially at weddings. The ambition of Dr. Newton, and the recollection of the scenes of his last visit at home, made him very cautious; and for some months he was successful in resisting his appetite. At length however he was overcome. It was at a wedding-party, where he drank wine (mark that, readers) *with the clergyman and his deacons.* The next morning beheld him a chagrined and wretched man. He felt too his own weakness even more than he did after his interview with his sister over his mother's grave. Still he did not yet come to the point of reliance on a higher power, but set to fortifying himself against the enemy with just those defences and those only, which had so often and so easily been broken down—and again, he dreamed of security. It was but a dream, and a short one too.

In the first rank of society in S— there was one man, Col. Dayton, a licentious bachelor, who exerted a vast influence, especially upon the young men. Although in the sober estimation of the good, he was perfectly vile and unprincipled, his manners were so popular, his address so fine, and his conversation was so full of anecdote and wit, and all this with a generous disposition, that he was considered a very amusing addition to any company, and was admitted freely even into families of a religious character. He was a very polite man, and had a show of artful frankness in his manner which deceived even the acutely discerning. He had been the ruin of a large number of young men. Though he was never known to be actually drunk himself, he has been the means of making many drunkards.

To Dr. Newton he was very attentive; and though his attentions were for some time not reciprocated beyond mere civility, from the insight which he at first had of his character, the tempter did at length succeed by his arts in drawing the victim within the circle of his influence. Dr. Newton was intimate with Col. Dayton before he knew it. This made his downfall certain. It brought him into contact with temptation continually, and, although his ambition excited by his success in business, his regard for his reputation, and his recollection of his vows and the warning voice of his sister, restrained him, his seasons of debauch became more and more frequent and worse in character, and soon the brandy bottle was his constant companion. Absolute sottishness came now with rapid stride, and in two years from the time that he came to S—, he left there in disgrace, a *wanderer*. So he continued to be for many years. Occasionally he went to his native place, and the entreaties of his sister would often for a little time have some effect upon him; but so easily did he yield to the every-where present temptation, that this effect, however promising it might appear, was but for a moment. After the most affecting interviews, when vows and promises were made with tears, the very next day, perhaps the next hour, would find him in a dram-shop.

At last he came to that horrid point,[20] which drunkards sometimes come to,—the point of perfect desperation. At the close of an interview with his sister, in which her entreaties drew not out, as they were wont, promises and tears, he thus burst forth—"It's of no use, Maria. I'm a drunkard, beyond all hope. I want to stop drinking, but I cannot—I *cannot*. I'm *chained* to death and destruction, and nothing can break that chain. Your entreaties and advice and prayers are all in vain. Pray for me no more—leave me to myself. I'm lost— lost."—As he uttered these words with the deliberate tone of a mind made up absolutely and finally, despair gave to his haggard, loathsome countenance a wild demoniac look, and his sister shuddered as she looked upon his glaring eye, and horror seemed to curdle the blood in her veins, and hope almost died in her bosom that had so long cherished it—*almost*, I say, but not quite—the fire was still there in the dying embers, to be fanned again by piety and faith and a sister's doating love—even now^ though it flickered almost to a solitary spark, in a moment it brightened up again—the shudder passed off—in a twinkling

---

20   Big Book, pg. 59 "We stood at the turning point."

she was reassured in her hope—her relaxing, trembling grasp of his hand became firm again, and in melting tones she said—"Oh brother, don't say so—prayer may yet avail—it must—it will"—and she sprang to his embrace.—

With a rude hand he thrust her off, saying with the same fixed air of desperation, "No—No—I'm lost"—and he rushed from her presence.

In what a tumult were now his feelings. A dozen times he was prompted to go back to that faithful sister, but the remembrance of the many times he had been melted down by her sweet influence, *and all in vain*, checked the rising purpose; and on he went with hurried step, till the open door of a dram-shop in the outskirts of the place invited him in. There he drowned the agitation of his bosom in beastly drunkenness. From this time he kept the very lowest company, and performed the most menial services to obtain the means of gratifying his appetite. My first acquaintance with him was as the hostler of Mr. Branson, in which office I first introduced him to the reader.

The first time that I saw him was in an open field. Though he was covered with rags, I at once perceived that in his air, which convinced me that he was the wreck of something noble and great. I had many conversations with him about his habits; but though he was often thoughtful and sometimes communicative, I could not dispossess him of the idea that his case was irretrievably lost. I did not despair, however, of ultimately doing so, for my nope was upheld by the fact, that I was once as really a slave to my appetite as poor Newton was now to his. I therefore followed him up with argument and entreaty every time that I met him.

At length he was attacked with delirium tremens. I spent three days and nights at Mr. Branson's tavern taking care of him. It was a sad sickness. But Mr. Branson seemed to think no more of it than he would of sickness of an ordinary kind. The ludicrous phantasies of the restless patient were matter of merriment to him—so surely does the business of selling rum destroy all kind feelings, all humanity in the bosom of him who pursues it for any length of time.

I shall never forget one night that I spent by his bed-side. It was a dreadful night. The rain fell in torrents, and the wind howled gloomily or blew in gusts. But the storm without was naught to the storm we witnessed within. The poor maniac saw all sorts of visions, the most ludicrous, and the most painful, all mixed up together. At one moment, for instance, he was convulsed with laughter at the dancing of cats, dogs, monkeys, and so forth, and cracked his jokes on the little monkey that fiddled for them—the next moment he was the very personification of terror, because he saw a throng of devils coming to torment him before his time. One of the devils was shod with skulls, and when he saw that devil of devils, as he called him, coming, he would shrink away into a corner, and with blanched face, and his eyes starting out from their sockets, and his teeth chattering, and his whole body trembling like an aspen leaf, he would say with a low unearthly whisper, "See him, see him—hear him clatter, clatter, clatter"—and then he would shriek out "Oh! Ohl Oh!"—and fall down for the moment senseless.

I thought he would die. And O what a death! To have reason dethroned, and the soul delivered over to the tortures conjured up by wild fancy—to be affrighted at every movement, every noise, even the whisper of kind friends,—to see foes, nay, demons, wherever the eye turns, to hear them on every side, ready to inflict their torture—to feel that torture crushing, pinching, biting, tearing, burning—thus to show forth in palpable shape the sufferings of the hell to which the Bible dooms the drunkard—and then to die and go to that hell—what a death! Rum-seller, what a death! Is it not enough to frighten you from your horrid business? Drunkard, what a death! But you are in danger of dying such a death every day of your life.—Moderate drinker, what a death! But every man that has died such a death was once like you, a moderate drinker.

He did not die. Blessed be God, he did not die. He recovered. One day as I sat by his bed-side I said to him—"You have been very sick—we thought for. several days that you would die, but God has spared you, and I believe that he has done it for some great purpose." Just at this moment a boy entered ringing a letter addressed to him. It was from his sister. As he read it he cried like a child. It ran thus—

"My dear Brother,

"You know not what anxiety I have felt about you since you left N—. I have not been able till to-day to find out where you had gone. With a full heart I sit down to write to you. You know how I have loved you, my only brother, and whenever you have escaped from the tyrant intemperance, you have reciprocated that love as an only brother should. You remember how with tears you have often promised me that you would reform, but temptation has again and again overcome you. But I have never given you up. No, dear William, a sister's love, and faith in God, have prompted me to follow you in your wanderings, with prayers and tears and entreaties. And now I feel a renewed zeal to labour for your recovery. So many have lately reformed who were as bad slaves to intemperance as you ever were, that every hour to the day, and often in the night, I say to myself, would to God that my beloved William were also one. A Washington Society has been formed here, and among the members are your friends, John Branch, Joseph Fowler, Charles Stone, and even old James Clark. If such men reform, why cannot you too? How happy should I be if I could only see you a sober man! What a brother you would then be to me. Your generous nature, your talents, your social qualities, now made a wreck by intemperance, if they could be restored, what a restoration? And it can be done. O try again. Come to me. Let me see you once more and talk with you about it. I know that I can persuade you now, and your friends here that nave reformed will help me too. They seem to be as happy as if they had escaped from prison, or even death. O come and be just as happy as they are. Do not delay. I shall count the hours till you come.

Your only sister, MARIA."

I have not space nor time, to detail the conversation that followed the reading of this letter. Suffice it to say that Dr. Newton, before an hour had gone, with a trembling hand but a firm heart, signed the pledge. O the magic of that pledge! How many it has saved from destruction! How many it has exalted from the very filth and mire of drunkenness to posts of respectability and usefulness! How many it has snatched, as it did my friend Newton, from the very verge of the bottomless pit!

And what is the magic of this pledge? There is no mystery in it though its results are like the workings of magic, it is a very simple thing. Its power lies in this—it brings the resolution of the drunkard to a settled point and that too, a point at which he knows that thousands of drunkards, just like himself, have in these latter days effected their deliverance, the sound of whose rejoicings is ringing in his ears, every day and in every place, in the public meeting, by the fire-side, in the work-shop, yes, in the very streets. No marvel then, that longing for the same deliverance, the poor, enslaved drunkard desires to sign the pledge,—and when he has signed it, and the chains fall from him, and he feels the warm glow of freedom in his bosom, no marvel that he stands up like a man and proclaims his freedom, and holds his pledge aloft as his " declaration of independence," and calls upon all that are suffering the worse than iron bondage of intemperance, to come and, like him, be free—no marvel, that as one after another lifts up his voice, multitudes of every class every where, in city and village and hamlet, do arise and are made free, and that, as the throng of the redeemed goes on to increase, the song of triumph comes to us on every breeze, and swells louder and louder as it sweeps over the length and breadth of the land.

Dr. Newton, once the filthy, ragged, besotted hostler of the vile Mr. Branson, is now not only a reformed man, but a Christian. The prayers of that devoted sister, sent up for him to heaven like sweet incense for so many, many long years, have not been sent up in vain—they have been heard and answered—arid what an answer!— an eternity of joy, of which they have now together the blessed foretaste. A happier hour I never spent than that when I presented to that astonished sister her brother, the lost but now found, "clothed and in his right mind." That scene I could not describe if I would. Little was said at first but we wept together tears of joy. There is truth in the saying "that rapture is born dumb."[21]

Yours, &c.

No. X.

MY friend Wilson and I lately visited Norwich, where, the reader will recollect, we became acquainted with each other. Of course we went to that Alms-house, from which I wrote my letters. It was a rainy day and we found the men all in doors picking oakum. It reminded me at once of the temperance discussion which we had five years ago in that same room, and which the reader will find described in No. VI. of Letters from the Alms-house. Some of the same characters were there. There sat Capt. Pepper, with the same big red nose, dealing out his wisdom from the large orifice under it, to the little knot around him. He was descanting upon the advice of Paul to Timothy, that favourite text of all that drink or sell intoxicating liquors, from the genteel-wine-drinker and respectable wholesale dealer, down to the filthy and ragged pauper. Just as we entered he was saying, "Ah, St. Paul knew what was good when he gave that advice to Timothy." "That's grammatically spoken," uttered a cracked voice, followed by a faint chuckle, and then a distressing cough. It was the voice of our old friend Dilly; there he sat, not picking oakum as he used to do with nimble fingers, when Wilson and I were his companions in this occupation, but bent over, pale and emaciated, with the lack-lustre of slowly approaching death in his little black eye, once so animated and restless.

I immediately went up to Captain Pepper, and introduced myself as an old acquaintance. At first, he did not recognize me. "Why," said I, "Captain, five years ago I sat here in this room by your side picking oakum." "Lord, bless me," cried he, eying me from head to foot, "and such a gentleman, now! Why, it can't be so." But I soon made him recollect both myself and Wilson, by recalling some events that occurred there, when we were in-mates of the house. Old Dilly's eyes, too, lightened up with the recollection of by-gone scenes, and he greeted us, "I'm glad to see ye—I'm glad to see ye—ugh, ugh, ugh. I guess you've had good times since you have been here, ugh, ugh; but the capting and I have had hard times enough, ugh, ugh, ugh. We've been sick most all the time." "Yes," said the captain, "you know how I used to be troubled with that 'sipelas humour, Mr. Mather. I've got a great ulcer on my leg, that originated in this same 'sipelas humour, that I 'spose was born with me." "That humour, captain," said Wilson, "you remember, you and I used to differ a little about. I used to tell you it was a *sipping*, not a 'sipelas humour." Capt. Pepper's countenance began to show a little rising anger at this allusion, and his lips began to quiver for a reply; but Wilson's comical look, calling up to his recollection the old scenes, when he used to laugh so heartily at his "yarns" and repartees, softened down at once the captain's wrath, and he concluded the best way was to return joke for joke. "Ah, you rogue, you," said he, "you love fun as well as ever, Wilson; your *humour* sticks to you as close as mine does to me.—Come, give us one of your old stories now ?" "Yes, yes," said old Dilly, hitching his chair up a little nearer. A sailor is always ready to do others a service in any way almost. So, to please them, he told them a story, and if I could put Wilson on to paper, I would tell it to the reader, but I cannot— half of the story was in his attitudes and gestures and expressions of countenance. After they had got through with their long laugh over Wilson's story, I asked the captain what was the matter with his hands, which I saw were bundled up with bandages* "Eve had a hard time with them, Mr. Mather," said he, "and I'll tell you all about it On the 20th January," and he went on to tell a long story, with all the minutise that garrulous old drunkards are apt to put in, the amount of which was, that in coming home on that night, he had a "vartigo" come over him, and so he got bewildered, and lost his way and froze his fingers, that "the 'sipelas humour had attracted 'em," and the doctor said that he should probably have to take some of them off. "We old fellows have hard times enough," said he. "Why, Mr. Mather, we're getting to be pretty old, Mr. Dilworth and I, and it's time for us to have some of the often infarmities that is spoken of in the Bible, you know." "That's grammatically spoken, ugh, ugh, ugh—that's the natral, ugh, ugh, natral course of things," said Mr. Dilworth. "Well," said I, "I have been very well since I left off drinking." "Left off drinking!" said the captain, with an air of perfect contempt. "So have I left off a great many times, ha, ha, ha." And all the miserable occupants of that room echoed his loud laugh, just as they had been accustomed to do, some of them for years—even old Dilly laughed and coughed together at the thread-bare joke. "This temperance business," continued the captain, "I don't believe in. Its contrary to Scripter. I know by my own experance that sperit is a good creatur of God. Why I should have been in my grave long ago, if I did'nt drink a little—a *little*, I say, just to keep soul and body together." "That's grammatically spoken," cried Mr. Dilworth, "ugh, a little would do me good now, ugh, ugh, ugh."

So talked these old topers, standing on the very brink of the drunkard's grave, using precisely the same arguments, or rather assertions, that are used by the moderate drinker—a little, a little—so say they all—a *little* is good. O, what multitudes of strong men that *little* has destroyed!

I found a much smaller number in the Almshouse, than were there when I was an inmate. There were only twenty-five, and that in the winter too. Some years ago, when the population of the town was but a little more than half what it is now, the number of inmates was between forty and fifty, and it has been as high as sixty. Nearly all that are there now were made paupers by intemperance; and when these are gone, the family at the Alms-house will be a very small one, perhaps so small that it will be advisable to break up the establishment, and board out the few poor and decrepit, who chance to have no relations to take care of them.

After leaving the Alms-house, we wandered about the streets of that beautiful and romantic town, which were once for a little time' the scene of our drunken misdeeds. Its rail-road has built up wonderfully, and the evidence of thrift is every where to be seen. We saw new houses' going up in every direction, and old ones were undergoing repairs, to lessen the contrast between them and their new neighbours. But all this, pleasing as it is, did not interest us so much as the change which has been effected there in regard to temperance. We found a goodly number of Washingtonians in Norwich, hard at work, adding constantly new recruits to their ranks. Some of them we recognized as old grog-shop acquaintances, that we fell in with during our former visit there. We found, too, that some of the rum sellers, at whose shops we drank at that time, have now given up the traffic, that others are talking about doing so, and that all of them say, that their business has fallen off astonishingly. In short, the same change is going on there that is going on in a thousand other places, scattering with a wide-cast prosperity and joy, and binding up multitudes of broken hearts.

And here the inquiry arises, is there any thing to hinder this reformation from spreading *every where*? I see not why the great principles on which it is based are not applicable to any people. Wherever there are drunkards, they can be operated upon by the same means that have been so successful in all places where they have been faithfully used. Would that I could make my voice heard throughout this land—I would call upon all the wise and good to rouse themselves, and bless the communities in which they live by the simple but wonder-working means of this great reformation.

Another interesting inquiry suggests itself. To what extent and at what rate is this reformation to succeed? Some in their enthusiasm talk of the *final* triumph of temperance, as if it were close at hand. But this is a mistaken view of the subject. As long as there are bad men, there will be intemperance. As long as there is vice, the great stimulator to vice will exist, and will have its votaries, and intemperance will always be one of the means, to which vicious men will resort, to silence and stupify conscience. It will remain then upon the earth to curse it as long as sin will—the final and complete triumph of temperance will not be realized till the dawn of the millennial day. But though we cannot at present effect the *total* destruction of intemperance, we can cripple its power, and limit its ravages, and drive it from the open walks of social intercourse, where it has so long held up a bold and shameless front, into dark and secret haunts, where it will be glad to flee, like other vices, from the light of day and the force of law. All this we are doing, and at a rapid rate. We are in the very midst of this great social transformation (for so it may be called,) *and the end is not yet—the day of these wonders has but begun.* Well may those who are engaged in the unholy traffic of alcohol fear and quake, for the time will soon come, when they can pursue this business only in the *secret* places of wickedness, in the very dens and caves of the earth.

Here, I should like to dwell on the agencies which are necessary to the permanence of this reformation. They have been pretty
fully illustrated in the "*Recollections*," which I have presented to
the reader, and my limits will, not allow me now only to hint at
them. They are principally these: 1. Religious sentiment. This must
be not only the chief, but the controlling agent. 2. Sympathy and
associated action. This is a powerful agent, or rather set of agencies,
but there is some danger of relying upon them too exclusively. 3.
Employment. I use this term in its widest sense. All the powers of
the reformed man, moral, intellectual and physical, must be direct-
ed into the proper channels of action. 4. Removal of temptation in
all its Protean forms. The principal obstacles to this are the cupidity
of the seller, the appetite of the buyer, and the customs of social life.

Many speak of the wonderful reformation that has been going
on during the past year, as if it were a thing of a year's growth. They
make no account of the efforts of the early friends of temperance;
some even speak disparagingly of them. But the change which
those efforts wrought in public sentiment, and in the customs of
Society, was *absolutely necessary* to prepare the community for the
present reformation. It could not have been successful—nay more,
it could not have been, unless this preparation, which has been going
on gradually, but surely, for years past, had preceded it. The early
friends of the cause cleared the ground—they drove in the plough-
share and dragged the harrow, and that too not lazily, but, as some
thought, rather too furiously,—they threw in the seed, and chased
away most industriously the flocks of foul birds that tried to pick
it up, and shot many of them with their* well-directed aim,—they
watched over the rising germs, and asked in faith for the fertilizing
dews and rains of heaven, and asked not in vain—for we are reaping
with them the golden harvest, and let us *with them* sing aloud the
song of the harvest-home.

Suppose that the little band, who began this reformation in Baltimore, had begun it twenty years ago. Even if it were possible for

them, with the customs then prevalent, and the state of feeling then existing in the community, to have persevered themselves in their attempt, it would have been confined mostly to them— they could not have extended their influence over the whole face of society, as they have now done. No. This *insurrection*, as it may well be called, among the subjects of king Alcohol,[22] would then most certainly have proved abortive.

The power of this monarch was then immense. He had armies of subjects bound to his standard by the strong tie of gold, and armies upon armies bound to it by the still stronger tie of appetite—his dominions how extensive!—his ships were on every sea—no tariff excluded his commodities from any country—all paid tribute to him, tribute too, which was often so oppressive as to bring to absolute want, and yet (so irresistible his magic power) paid willingly—his sway was almost undisputed, and he commanded the respect of the whole world, as one of the mightiest among the powers that be—poets had for ages sung of the enchantments of his throne and sceptre, and philosophers, and the great men of the earth had paid to them the homage of their admiration, and he fashioned to a great extent, the social customs of all people, in all countries and climes. A few, it is true, had dared to call him a tyrant, but their voice was drowned in the general acclamation of praise. Ah, an insurrection then! how futile! It would have been crushed in its very bud. It would have excited nothing but the passing notice of a sneer, and then would have been forgotten.

But how different the situation of things when this insurrection did take place. A constant and effectual war had been waged against this mighty king, for years, which had deprived him of a large portion of his dominions, and shorn him of much of his power—multitudes of his subjects had deserted him, and multitudes more, who were disposed to join his standard, had come out openly against him— the tribute paid to him was every day diminishing—the very foundations of his ancient throne were shaken—and besides all this, all the world, instead of praising him, as they once

---

22   Big Book, pg. 151 "As we became subjects of King Alcohol, shivering denizens of his mad realm, the chilling vapor that is loneliness settled down."

did, had come to speak evil of him, and he was almost everywhere boldly proclaimed a tyrant, so that he was not only a weakened, but a disgraced monarch—and thus stripped of the greatness of his might, and dispirited by defeat after defeat, and loss upon loss, and by the disgrace into which he had been plunged from his giddy height of glory, no wonder that an insurrection, begun in the very citadel (for the dram-shop is the citadel) of his empire, should now succeed, and threaten to hurl him from his throne. The war which is now going on against him, is a destructive one. This once vast and mighty kingdom is fast dwindling away. It will ere long become a mere little piratical power, prowling about in secret for its spoils, proscribed by the laws of all civilized nations as a common enemy, to be hunted from the face of the earth. Well may we exclaim, how has the mighty fallen!

With this number I close my Recollections. I do not stop from lack of material. The experience I have had, first of the woes of intemperance, for many, many long years, and then of the joys of the reformed man for the past two years of my life, and my intercourse with others who have suffered the same woes, and have at length come into the possession of the same joys, furnish me with almost an exhaustless stock of interesting and instructive facts.[23] From these I have culled such portions as I thought would best show the temptations which endanger the reformed man, and illustrate the movements and principles of the present wonderful reformation.

When I came out of the Alms-house, I offered to deliver some lectures on temperance, if any body would furnish me with a decent suit of clothes; and I really believe that if any one would have done this for me, I should have been a fully reformed man at that time. The time had not come however for such effort then, but the proposition which I made, and which was then laughed at, is now practised upon extensively, and some of our most efficient lecturers have been taken from Alms-houses, and Houses of Correction, and

23   Big Book, pg. 89. "Life will take on new meaning. To watch people recover, to see them help others, to watch loneliness vanish, to see a fellowship grow up about you, to have a host of friends - this is an experience you must not miss. We know you will not want to miss it. Frequent contact with newcomers and with each other is the bright spot of our lives."

even Prisons. When I made that proposition, it was not really in earnest; I did not dream that I ever should be a lecturer on temperance, or that I should ever speak through the press, to any body else than the readers of the periodical, in which my *Letters from the Alms-house* were originally published. If I have done any good to the glorious cause of temperance; if I have waked up any to greater energy and zeal in labouring for this cause; above all, if I have been the instrument of rescuing any from the degradation and misery of intemperance, I am glad that these humble efforts of mine have been presented to the public. In conclusion, let me say—Reader, be not a mere spectator, but an active labourer in the wide field of this reformation. "Whatsoever thy hand findeth to do, do it with thy might," for surely this field is "white already to harvest"[24]

THE END.

---

[24]   Ecclesiastes 9:10 "Whatsoever thy hand findeth to do, do it with thy might; for there is no work, nor device, nor knowledge, nor wisdom, in the grave, whither thou goest." John 4:35 "Say not ye, There are yet four months, and then cometh harvest? behold, I say unto you, Lift up your eyes, and look on the fields; for they are white already to harvest."

APPENDIX A:
THE DREAM:
OR
THE TRUE HISTORY
OF
DEACON GILES'S DISTILLERY,
AND
DEACON JONES'S BREWERY.
By Rev. GEO. B. CHEEVER, D. D.

Publisher Note: We have decided to include these two short narratives, and the introduction preceding them, because the author alluded to them in an offhand way, implying his Readership would be familiar with it. It is poetic allegory in the vein of Bunyan, Dante, or Blake.

INTRODUCTION.

A republication of this remarkable production, seems called for at the present time, when, from many sections of our country, the complaint is heard, that the tide of intemperance, which for a time had been checked, is beginning to rise again, and overflow communities that had been, in a measure, reclaimed from it. For the information of the reader, some account of its origin, is here prefixed, which we extract from a "History," prepared for a former Edition, by Rev. John Marsh, D. D., Corresponding Secretary of the American Temperance Union.

"The Rev. George B. Cheever was at this time a young minister in Salem, Mass. He had commenced his ministry with an uncompromising spirit toward whatever hindered the spread of the Gospel kingdom. He often passed those murky establishments where, day and night, Sabbath and week days, the lurid fires were burning, and the horrid machinery was in motion. From four distilleries there, no less than six hundred thousand gallons of ardent spirits were annually poured forth; through whose instrumentality, it was believed, a thousand individuals were reduced to pauperism, and four hundred were sent to the drunkard's grave. Of three thousand persons admitted to the work-house within a few minutes' walk of his study, two thousand nine hundred were brought there, directly or indirectly, through intemperance. Over these evils, and an untold corruption of public sentiment, desecration of the Sabbath, and ruin of souls connected with them, lie could not sleep. And if he slept he dreamed. He dreamed "a dream, which was not all a dream."

"Inquire at Amos Giles's Distillery."

Upon its appearance in the Salem Landmark, of February, 1835, the public excitement was tremendous. Every distiller and importer, every vender and moderate drinker, almost the entire community, believing that what was legally right, must yet be respected and honored, how horrid soever might be its moral results, cried out against it as an outrage upon society. "With one accord, they rushed to the halls of justice for protection.—Among the four distilleries of the place, one was singled out as answering more directly to the description; and the proprietor, himself a Deacon of a Christian Church, and a man of unexceptionable character, feeling aggrieved and injured in his person and property, a prosecution was commenced by the Commonwealth for a libel. Mr. Cheever pleaded not guilty to the charge, solemnly averring that it was never written or intended as an attack upon any individual; the object of the piece was to portray, in as forcible a light as possible, through the medium of the fiction he had conceived, the real nature and consequences of the manufacture of ardent spirits. "If any man (said Mr. Cheever.) is at a loss for a motive to the publication of the article, let him contemplate for a moment the nature of the traffic in ardent spirits. Let him cast his eyes over the vast catalogue of human crime and misery. There are no enormities which the business of distilling does not produce, no extravagances of iniquity to which it does not lead. It is literally the wholesale manufacturer of iniquity of every description. It would challenge the ingenuity of mankind to show that it is anything else. I stand here accused of crime in attacking a trade which in itself is the production of all crime, and has occasioned more criminal litigation than all other causes. I stand here accused of violating the laws of my country in attacking a business whose direct, inevitable, supreme, and incessant result, is the trampling under foot, and defiance, and destruction of all law and all obligation, human and divine. I am here to answer to a charge of defaming the character, and wantonly and maliciously injuring the peace, of families and individuals, in vividly depicting an employment which is nothing but ruin to the character, and death to the peace, temporal and eternal, of thousands of families, and hundreds of thousands of individuals. I am arraigned as a criminal at this bar for disturbing the peace of the Commonwealth, and the domestic happiness of its households, in attacking a business whose positive, unchangeable operation is to till the Commonwealth with brawls, riots, robberies, murders, and its households with drunkenness, wrath, poverty, and anguish. You can not show that the business of distilling is anything else. It tends to break up all social order, prostrate all barriers of law, set fire to all violent human passions, and whelm all institutions of blessedness, domestic, civil, and religious, in one blasting, fiery tide of ruin. It leaves no man's character, no man's property, no man's family, safe. I stand here accused of crime in attacking this infernal traffic, and painting its consequences in colors but too faithful to the life.

"That I may not seem to your honor to be dealing in declamation, and that you may have fully before your mind the motive that actuated my efforts, let me here refresh your memory with some of the dreadful statistics dependent on the existence and activity of the distillery. They are statistics of misery, uninterrupted in their recurrence and accumulation, in authenticated estimates, catalogues, and certificates, of the wreck of property and character, and the spread of pauperism, crime, disease, and death. On a calculation taken from one of the most temperate communities, by actual census of the counties of Wayne and Seneca, and five towns in Cayuga county, in the state of New York, and showing one drunkard to every twenty-seven inhabitants, in the fourteen millions of our country, there are at this day more than five hundred thousand drunkards in the United States. Are we startled at the fact? There is nothing speculative in the statement. The returns were made from actual examination, by competent, respectable men, and the particulars of each town were given separately. Does the result seem incredible? Surely we do not meet an intoxicated wretch in every twenty-seven individuals. We may not meet them in our daily walks and occupations. They are not commonly out in the face of the community, and we well know they are not an active, enterprising race. Their very habits exclude them from the sweet light and the wholesome business of society. Theirs are the abodes of filth and raggedness, the homes that they fill with guilt and anguish. Part people our alms-houses and prisons. Part line our canals, and crowd the hidden, impure, and almost subterranean streets of our cities. They inhabit the dens and caves of civilization, the pest-haunts of sin, the cellars, and bar-rooms, and grog-shops. There they congregate; there they inflame their passions, and profane the name of God. But on every occasion of brawls and riots, whenever deeds of wickedness are in progress, or the elements of a mob have opportunity and space for combination, then they emerge from their darkness, and your sight is arrested by savage faces and haggard forms, reeling and reeking from the hot hells, where the stream of the distillery is poured and drank at a thousand fountains.

"Consider next the fearful waste of life attendant on the prosecution of this horrid business. Of these live hundred thousand human beings, between fifty and sixty thousand die every year. Their places are supplied by an unfailing corps, who are passing hourly from the ranks of the so-called temperance drinkers, to the vast body of the intemperate. An immense procession to the grave is thus kept up, whose miserable conscripts are from all families; a stream of diseased and vicious human life, swollen from all classes in society, like the troubled sea, for protracted vice and anguish in this world, and poured annually into an eternal world of ruin!

"It seems little after this, to remind your honor of the national and individual pecuniary loss consequent on the successful business of the distillery. The Attorney-General of the United States has stated the annual loss to the Union from the use of ardent spirits to be one hundred millions of dollars. This statement is doubtless much within the truth: and calculations have been made, which show that directly and indirectly the amount lost is from one hundred and fifty to two hundred millions annually. It is more than enough, as computed by Judge Cranch, to buy up all the houses, lands, and slaves, in the United States every twenty years.

"The waste of money is nothing to the waste of mind; the loss of sound minds in sound bodies; the loss of so many temperate and intelligent mechanics, artisans, farmers, and professional men. who would otherwise go to swell the moral and intellectual power ot the nation; the loss of a thousand influences, hitherto swept onwards in a tide of ruin, that might have been a tide of blessing to the world. In all other ways there has never been such a waste of intellect and morals as by this one vice. It has brooded, like a mighty incubus of death, over our whole physical, intellectual, and moral system. The money lost is infinitely worse than if it had been annihilated, or taken from the mint and sunk in the ocean; for it is expended in the annual production of wretchedness and crime.

"Of the crime and pauperism connected with intemperance, and sustained by the business of the distillery, I may state that out of 25,707 individuals found in the poor-houses and jails in the city of New York in a single year, 21,553 were brought there directly or indirectly from intemperance. Estimating the people of New York at one-seventh of the population in this country, we have in the United States, 148,799 criminals and paupers, made such by the use of ardent spirits.

"Now, let me ask, Where rests the responsibility of this fearful accumulation of death and crime? It can not be doubted that it rests upon those who make and sell ardent spirits; for they know that that is the agent by which all this misery is produced. They know its destructive tendencies; they know that it is rank poison, in the class of narcotic, vegetable poisons, as sheer poison as henbane; they know that it kills the body and kills the soul They can not help knowing it; amidst all the light poured upon the subject, there is not a dramseller nor a distiller in the land but knows it.

"The distiller is generally wealthy. He must be rich, or he could not well be a distiller. He has not, therefore, even the poor apology, so often alleged for continuing in the traffic, that if he quits it his family must, suffer; an apology without foundation for any individual; for were he to shoulder a sawhorse, and saw wood from door to door for his subsistence, he would be a happier and healthier man, and his family a happier and healthier family. But the manufacturer has grown so rich in this dreadful business, that he could afford to burn down his distillery, and turn all his liquor into the streets, and still possess a competency. He might throw the whole investment into the ocean, and still command ample capital to enter upon any honest livelihood whatever. He is more guilty in continuing this traffic than any dramseller in the land. Yet while the business of dramselliag may be attacked, and the community applaud the exposer, the business of distilling, the source of the whole evil, shall be comparatively shielded; and if a man advers to the fact in the history of a distiller—if he speak of the monstrous conjunction of rum and Bibles in one and the same manufactory—he shall first be assaulted in the streets, and then prosecuted for libel; while the men who outraged the law in assaulting him shall be loaded with applause, and, with one exception, dismissed from, court without even the form of a trial, at the discretion of the same public officer who conducts the libel prosecution against the individual already subjected to that violence.

"I am not willing to believe that your honor will tend your influence to sanction this enormity.—You will see that the respectability of the distiller can with no more propriety shield his occupation from scorn, than that of the dramseller can protect his. He may boast in his veins the blood of all the Howards, or he may have descended from the man who first put a bottle to the lips of his neighbor; his family may be rich and respectable, or poor and degraded; he may be a member of the church, receiving on the Sabbath, the emblems of the body and blood of his Saviour, with the same hands that during the week prepare and circulate the means for his betrayal; or he may be a man excommunicated from the church for persisting in the traffic in ardent spirits: whether he be the one or the other, is to you a matter of entire indifference. You will remember that 'it is just because the sin of intemperance is upheld by the rich and reputable, and by professed Christians that Temperance Reform drays so heavily.'

"In mitigation of judgment at this time," he said, "I need scarcely remind your honor more particularly of the course taken by the Attorney-General in the discharge of two of the individuals engaged in the assault upon my person, without even the form of trial. Whether it be a greater offence in the judgment of this court to describe a distiller's occupation, as I have done in the *Landmark*; or with personal violence attack an unarmed citizen as they did in the street, the sentence which may be declared will go far to determine. I know not by what rule of justice the latter criminals, with proof clear, full, and conclusive against them, were suffered to depart triumphant in their violation of the law, while the former alleged offence has been prosecuted with such undeviating fixedness of purpose. It seems to me a singularly unjust proceeding.

"I solicit the favor of thy court upon manly grounds. I ask for an acquittal, because I am guiltless of the crime for which I am arraigned before you. I have assaulted no man's character—I have injured no man's family—I have committed no offence against the laws of my country. For the sake of freedom in the proclamation of truth. I am unwilling that an unrighteous and oppressive verdict should be sustained and sanctioned by the decision of this court. For the sake of justice, I am unwilling to be punished for a crime which I have never committed. For the sake of temperance. I am unwilling that the distillery interest, productive in this legion of such incalculable misery, should here find a shield.

"Could the amount of misery, in time and eternity, which any one distillery in Salem has occasioned, be portrayed before your honor, I should feel no solicitude for the result. Let mothers who have been broken-hearted, the wives that have been made widows, the children that have been made fatherless, the parents borne down with a bereavement worse than death, in the vices of their children, be arrayed in your presence: let the families reduced to penury, disgraced with crime, and consumed with anguish, that the owners of one distillery might accumulate their wealth be gathered before you. Let the prosecutor in this suit go to the grave-yards, and summon those whose bodies have been laid in the grave from that one distillery: let him call up, if he could, the souls that have been shut out from heaven and prepared for hell, through the instrumentality of the liquor manufactured there: and let them ask what, is their verdict. Need I suppose the judgment? Surely it would be said. Let the defendant be shielded. Even if he has overstepped the limits of exact prudence, in his efforts to portray the evils of intemperance, in the name of mercy, let the great object of the effort shield him, and let the law be turned against that dreadful business whose nature he has aimed to delineate."

Such, however, was the state of the public mind that he was condemned, and, on making his defence, he submitted meekly to the sentence of the Court. But the whole procedure gave wings to the production of his genius, and caused it to become one of the great instruments of opening the eyes of a suffering community to the true character of distillation.

The history of this transaction forms a part of the history of the Temperance Reformation. While it presents to posterity one of those signal incidents by which the mighty enginery of drunkenness has been nearly overthrown, it reflects nothing upon those who then felt themselves injured, both in their good name and worldly prosperity. The darkness that overshadowed them and the community in which they dwelt, is the apology for their faults. Haply it may be, that they are now foremost in the condemnation of the business whose character was exposed. The old distillery has long since been abandoned, and the building, now converted to useful purposes, was recently the scene of a joyful Temperance tea party.

Autobiography Of
(For the Salem Landmark)
"INQUIRE AT AMOS GILES'S DISTILLERY."

Some time ago the writer's notice was arrested by an advertisement in one of the newspapers, which closed with words similar to the following: "Inquire at Amos Giles's Distillery." The reader may suppose, if he choose, that the following story was a dream, suggested by that phrase.

Deacon Giles was a man who loved money, and was never troubled with tenderness of conscience. His father and his grandfather before him had been distillers, and the same occupation had come to him as an heir-loom in the family. The still-house was black with age, as well as with the smoke of furnaces that never went out, and the fumes of tortured ingredients, ceaselessly converted into alcohol. It looked like one of Vulcan's Stithies, translated from the infernal regions into this world. Its stench filled the atmosphere, and it seemed as if drops of poisonous alcoholic perspiration might be made to ooze out from any one of its timbers or clapboards at a slight pressure. Its owner was a treasurer to a Bible Society; and he had a little counting-room in one corner of the distillery where he sold Bibles.

He that is greedy of gain, troubleth his own house. Any one of those Bibles might have told him this, but he chose to learn it from experience. It was said that the Worm of the Still lay coiled in the bosom of his family; and certain it is that one of its members had drowned himself in a vat of hot liquor, in the bottom of which a skeleton was some time after found, with heavy weight tied to the ankle bones. Moreover, Deacon Giles's temper was none of the sweetest naturally; and the liquor he drank, and the fires and spirituous fumes among which he lived, did nothing to soften it. If his workmen sometimes fell into his vats, he himself oftener fell out with his workmen. This was not to be wondered at, considering the nature of their wages, which, according to no unfrequent stipulation, would be as much raw rum as they could drink.

Deacon Giles worked on the Sabbath. He would neither suffer

the fires of the distillery to go out, or to burn while he was idle; so he kept as busy as they. One Saturday afternoon his workmen had quarrelled, and all went off in anger. He was in much perplexity for want of hands to do the work of the devil on the Lord's day. In the dusk of the evening a gang of singular-looking fellows entered the door of the distillery. Their dress was wild and uncouth, their eyes glared, and their language had a tone that was awful. They offered to work for the Deacon; and he, on his part, was overjoyed, for he thought within himself that, as they had probably been turned out of employment elsewhere, he could engage them on his own terms.

He made them his accustomed offer, as much ruin every day, when the work was done, as they could drink; but they would not, take it. Some of them broke out and told him that they had enough of hot things where they came from, without drinking damnation in the distillery. And when they said that, it seemed to the Deacon as if their breath burned blue; but he was not certain, and could not tell what to make of it. Then he offered them a pittance of money; but they set up such a laugh, that he thought the roof of the building would fall in. They demanded a sum which the deacon said he could not give, and would not, to the best set of workmen that ever lived, much less to such piratical-looking scape jails as they. Finally, he said, he would give half what they asked, if they would take two-thirds of that in Bibles. When he mentioned the word Bibles, they all looked towards the door, and made a step backwards, and the Deacon thought they trembled; but whether it was with anger or delirium tremens, or something else, he could not tell. However, they winked, and made signs to each other, and then one of them, who seemed to be the head man, agreed with the Deacon, that if he would let them work by night instead of day, they would stay with him awhile and work on his own terms. To this he agreed, and they immediately went to work.

The Deacon had a fresh cargo of molasses to be worked up, and a great many hogsheads then in from his country customers, to be filled with liquor. When he went home he locked up the doors, leaving the distillery to his new workmen. As soon as he was gone, you would have thought that one of the chambers of hell had been transported to earth with all its inmates. The distillery glowed with fires and burned hotter than ever before; and the figures of the demons passing to and fro, and leaping and yelling in the midst of their work, made it look like the entrance to the bottomless pit.

Some of them sat astride the rafters, over the heads of the others, and amused themselves with blowing flames out of their mouths. The work of distilling seamed play to them, and they carried it on with supernatural rapidity. It was hot enough to have boiled the molasses in any part of the distillery; but they did not seem to mind it at all. Some lifted the hogsheads as easily as you would raise a tea cup, and turned their contents into the proper receptacles; some scummed the boiling liquids; some, with huge ladles, dipped the smoking fluid from the different vats, and raising it high in the air, seemed to take great, delight in watching the fiery stream, as they spouted it back again; some drafted the distilled liquor into empty casks and hogsheads; some stirred the tires; all were boisterous and horribly profane, and seemed to engage in their work with such familiar and malignant satisfaction, that I conclud-ed the business of distilling was as natural as hell, and must have originated there. I gathered from their talk that they were going to play a trick upon the Deacon, that should cure him of offering rum and Bibles to his workmen; and I soon found out from their conversation and movements what it was. They were going to write certain inscriptions on all his rum casks, that should remain invis-ible until they were sold by the Deacon, but should flame out in characters of fire as soon as they were broached by his retailers, or exposed to the use of the drunkards.

When they had filled a few casks with liquor, one of them took a great coal of fire, and having quenched it in a mixture of rum and molassses, proceeded to write, apparently by way of experiment, upon the heads of the different vessels. Just as it was dawn, they left off work, and all vanished together.

In the morning the Deacon was puzzled to know how the workmen got out of the, distillery, which he found fast locked as he had left it. He was still more amazed to find that they had done more work in one night, than could havo been accomplished, in the ordinary way, in three weeks. He pondered the things not a little, and almost concluded that it was the work of supernatural agents. At any rate, they had done so much that he thought he could afford to attend meeting that day, as it was the Sabbath. Accordingly he went to church, and heard his minister say that God could pardon sin without an atonement, that the words hell and devil were mere figures of speech, and that all men would certainly be saved. He was much pleased, and inwardly resolved that he would send his minister a half cask of wine; and as it happened to be communion Sabbath, he attended meeting all day.

In the evening the men came again, and again the Deacon locked them in to themselves, and they went to work. They finished all his molasses, and filled all his rum barrels, and kegs, and hogsheads, with liquor, and marked them all, as on the preceding night, with invisible inscriptions. Most of the titles ran thus:

"Consumption sold here. Inquire at Deacon Giles's Distillery."

"Convulsions and epilepsies. Inquire at Amos Giles's Distillery."

"Insanity and murder. Inquire at Deacon Giles's Distillery."

"Dropsy and Rheumatism. Putrid Fever, and Cholera in the collapse. Inquire at Amos Giles's Distillery."

"Delirium Tremens. Inquire at Deacon Giles's Distillery."

Many of the casks had on them inscriptions like the following:
"Distilled Death and liquid Damnation."

"The Elixir of Hell for the bodies of those whose souls are coming there."

Some of the demons had even taken sentences from the Scriptures, and marked the hogsheads thus:
"Who hath wo? Inquire at Deacon Giles's Distillery."

"Who hath redness of eyes? Inquire at Deacon Giles's Distillery."

Others had written sentences like the following:
"A potion from the lake of fire and brimstone. Inquire at Deacon Giles's Distillery."

All these inscriptions burned, when visible, a "still and awful red." One of the most terrible in its appearance was as follows:

"Weeping and wailing and gnashing of teeth.

Enquire at Deacon Giles's Distillery."

In the morning the workmen vanished as before, just as it was dawn; but in the dusk of the evening they came again, and told the Deacon it was against their principles to take any wages for work done between Saturday night and Monday morning, and as they could not stay with him any longer, he was welcome to what they had done. The Deacon was very urgent to have them remain, and offered to hire them for the season at any wages, but they would not. So he thanked them and they went away, and he saw them no more. In the course of the week most of the casks were sent into the country, and duly hoisted on their stoups, in conspicuous situations, in the Taverns, and Groceries, and the Rum-shops. But no sooner had the first glass been drawn from any of them, than the invisible inscriptions flamed out on the cask-head to every beholder. "**CONSUMPTION SOLD HERE, DELIRIUM TREMEMS. DAMNATION AND HELL-FIRE.**"

The drunkards were terrified from the dram-shops; the bar-rooms were emptied of their customers: but in their place a gaping crowd filled every store that possessed a cask of the Deacon's devil-distilled liquor, to wonder and be affrighted at the spectacle. For no art could efface the inscriptions. And even when the liquor was drawn into new casks, the same deadly letters broke out in blue and red flames all over the surface.

The rumsellers, and grocers, and tavern-keepers, were full of fury. They loaded their teams with the accursed liquor, and drove it back to the distillery. All around and before the door of the Deacon's establishment the returned casks were piled one upon another, and it seemed as if the inscriptions burned brighter than ever. Consumption, Damnation, Death, and Hell, mingled together in frightful confusion; and in equal prominence, in every case. flamed out the direction,

"INQUIRE AT DEACON GILES'S DISTILLERY."

One would have thought that the bare sight would have been

enough to terrify every drunkard from his cups, and every trader from the dreadful traffic in ardent spirits. Indeed, it had some effect for a time, but it was not lasting, and the demons knew it would not be, when they played the trick: for they knew the Deacon would continue to make rum, and that as long as he continued to make it, there would be people to buy and drink it. And so it proved.

The Deacon had to turn a vast quantity of liquor into the streets, and burn up the hogsheads; and his distillery has smelled of brimstone ever since; but he would not give up the trade. He carries it on still; and every time I see his advertisement, "Inquire at Amos Giles's Distillery," I think I see Hell and Damnation, and he the proprietor.

Autobiography Of

DEACON JONES'S BREWERY.

"You will be doing my work."— Demon.

Deacon Jones, from early life, had been a distiller of New England rum. He entered on the business when everybody thought it was a calling as honest as the miller's, and he grew rich by it. But the nature of his occupation, and the wealth he was gaining, sadly seared his conscience. Of seven promising sons, three had died drunkards, two were lost at sea in a vessel whose cargo was rum from the Deacon's own distillery, and two were living at home, idle and dissipated. Yet it never occurred to the father that he himself had been the cause of all this misery to his own family; he was even wont to converse with great resignation on the subject of his trials, declaring that he found comfort in the passage that reads that "whom the Lord loveth he chasteneth, and scourgeth every son whom he receiveth." His business was very extensive, and he plied the trade of death with unremitting assiduity.

When the Temperance Reformation commenced, Deacon Jones took ground against it. He declared it was a great piece of fanaticism. He was once heard to say, that if the bones of his ancestors could rattle in their graves, it would be to hear the business of distilling denounced as productive of death to men's bodies, and damnation to their souls. The progress of the reformation was so rapid, that at length he began to see that it must, in the end. greatly injure his business, and curtail his profits. Moreover, he did not feel easy on the score of conscience, and when the members of the Church proceeded to excommunicate a dramseller, who kept his grog-shop open on the Sabbath, and had been in the habit of procuring all his supplies at the Deacon's distillery, he trembled, lest his brethren should take it into their heads that the business of distilling was the foundation of the whole evil. It was said that he was much disturbed by an article in the newspaper which came strongly under his notice, descriptive of the immorality of the business of the distiller, and ending with these words: "I think I see hell and damnation, and he the proprietor" For a long time the Deacon

A Reformed Drunkard

could not enter his distillery, without thinking of those dreadful words; he considered them so profane, that he thought the article ought to be presented as a nuisance by the Grand Jury.

At length the perplexities of conscience, and the fears of self-interest, drove him to think seriously of emitting the business. One afternoon, as he was sitting at home, absorbed in thought, a loud, impetuous knock at the door of the apartment, startled him, and in walked one of the most singular personages he ever remembered to have seen. It was a man apparently about fifty years of age, very short of stature and sturdy in bulk, with a countenance that indicated uncommon shrewdness, and an eye of preternatural brilliancy and power. Yet his features were extremely irregular, and so evidently marked with strong but compressed passion, as to put one in mind of the crater of a hushed volcano; in fact, his face, in some positions, almost wore the aspect of a fiend escaped from the infernal regions. With all this, he could assume, if he chose, a strange, incongruous appearance of humor; his countenance had that expression when he entered the room where the Deacon was meditating.

He had on a coat of blue broadcloth, of the fashion of Queen Anne's age, a white satin waistcoat with enormous flaps covered with figures of dancing satyrs wrought in crimson silk, and pantaloons of red velvet, over which was drawn a pair of white topped boots, that reached nearly to his knees, with feet of extraordinary magnitude. On his head was a three-cornered adjutant's hat, which lie raised with an easy bow as he entered. His salutation to the Deacon was kindly expressed, though in a very deep, startling voice, that seemed as if it came almost from the centre of the earth. He told the Deacon he was happy to see him, and knowing that he was somewhat troubled in mind, he had called to help him out of his perplexities.

The Deacon looked uneasy at this address, and told his visitor that he did not remember ever to have seen him. Upon that the man laughed very extravagantly, and confessed it was not strange that he did not recognize him: "but no matter for that." said he, "I think I can certainly assure you that I am without doubt the best friend you have in the world."

The Deacon did not care to contradict him, especially as his face just then looked strangely malignant; so he proceeded to draw the Deacon into a long conversation, in which the man in blue and velvet seemed an adept in the mystery of distilling, and a friend to the art. The Deacon told him all his trouble in regard to the Temperance Reformation. "Not," said he, "that I dislike the thing itself, in the abstract. I am as firm a temperance man as any one. But really they do adopt such hot-headed fanatical measures, and are carrying the thing to such an extreme, that it is enough to put one out of all patience. It is not strange that even good people should be driven to oppose the reformation in mere self-defense. I am for temperance under the broad banner of the law; and the law protects the business of distilling as much as it does any business: in my view the making of rum is just as honest a calling as the making of gunpowder."

The man in blue acquiesced, and told the Deacon that he heartily hated these Anti-Societies for the purpose of putting down particular sins, and he said he thought a great deal more injury was done by intemperate writing than by intemperate drinking. Nevertheless he told him that he thought a brewery would be quite as profitable as a distillery, and that the business, moreover, would work in very well, just then, with the public mind, on the score of temperance. He proposed a visit to the Deacon's, distillery, and told him he thought, between them, they could contrive a new and convenient disposure of the whole establishment.

Accordingly, with this interesting conversation, they proceeded to the distillery, and after examining the premises, sat down in the Deacon's counting-room in which, it may be remarked, he kept a copy of Bangs on Distillation, but no Bibles. Here again they had a long conversation, after which the man in blue told the Deacon that if he would give over to him the care of the distillery for that night, he thought he could make it a good temperance speculation, and arrange matters perfectly to his mind. By this time the man seemed to have acquired a strange power over the Deacon, and he agreed to all his propositions without much delay. So the workmen retired to their homes at sundown, and the deacon to his, leaving the keys of the distillery and counting-room in his velvet friend's possession.

That night there was a violent thunder-storm, and the Deacon slept but little. Had he known the scenes that were transacting in his distillery, he would not have slept at all. The stage-man, who drove the mail, passed the distillery, which was situated on the main road, about midnight, and afterwards declared, that through the windows of the distillery, which he thought burned blue, he could see a crowd of wild and savage-looking creatures hurrying to and fro, and though it was thundering at a fearful rate, he could hear the strangest supernatural voices, amidst all the fury of the storm. This was probably not merely the man's excited imagination; for after the Deacon's departure, as night drew on, the distillery was filled with a troop of demoniacal-looking beings, who seemed ripe even for a midnight murder, and all under the control of the strange man left by the Deacon in the counting-room.

It was soon easy to perceive by their movements what was their object. With supernatural strength and dexterity they proceeded to disorganize the whole internal paraphernalia of the Deacon's establishment. They tore up and emptied all his vats, but carefully deposited the dregs and filth of distillation, wherever they found it, in a large muddy cistern, which they discovered conveniently disposed at one end of the distillery. They took in pieces the whole machinery of distillation, and by a wonderful metamorphosis, they so remodelled its parts and refitted the vats, as to make them admirably suited to the processes of malting and brewing. The worm of the still they uncoiled, and sheathed the bottom of the new vats with the lead that came out of it.

Some of them I observed were busy in bringing in and piling up huge bags of barley; others in constructing the furnaces and chambers where the malt was to be dried; others in filling the cisterns into which the dregs of the vats had been poured, with dirty water dipped from a stagnant pond, covered with green slime and infested with crawling reptiles, hard by the distillery. They set the barley for malt, and so peculiar were the qualities of the malting mixture in the cistern, and so admirable the skill with which they had prepared the furnace and floors for kiln-drying, that a process was accomplished in less than an hour, which ordinarily demanded some days for its completion. The task of mashing was an easy one, and the wort was drawn off and boiled down, and the coolers tilled, with surprising celerity: and, to crown all, they set the liquor for fermentation in a tun of prodigious dimensions, which one party had been engaged in constructing, while the others were busied in the process of malting, mashing, boiling, and cooling.

In the midst of all this astounding bustle, the man in the counting-room was neither idle, nor satisfied with the mere superintendence of his energetic workmen. He stripped off his broadcloth and velvet, disencumbered himself of his huge boots, and appeared the most gaunt, active, and demoniacal among the whole crew. They leaped, and grinned, and jibbered, and swore, in so terrific a manner, that it seemed as if the thunder, which was breaking in such tremendous artillery across the heavens, would have been charged to peal in among them, for their horrible profaneness.

But the most astonishing scene took place while they boiled down the liquor. They gathered in a double circle, and danced to music as infernal as the rhymes they chanted were malignant, amidst the bickering flames and smoke of the furnace, round about the huge copper cauldron of boiling liquid, into which each of them, from moment to moment, adapting the action to the words they sang, threw such ingredients as they had provided for the occasion. I shall scarcely be credited, while I relate what poisonous and nauseous drugs they cast into the agitated mixture. Opium, henbane, cocculus indicus, nux vomica, grains of paradise, and Bohemian rosemary; aloes, gentian, quassia, wormwood, and treacle; capsicum, cassia-buds, isinglass, cods-sounds, and oil of vitriol, were dashed in turn amidst the foaming mass of materials which they stirred and tasted, scalding hot as it was, with a ferocious exulting delight, that seemed to increase in proportion as the quality of its properties grew more pernicious. They could not but remind me of Shakspeare's witches, on the blasted heath at midnight, when the charm was brewing for Duncan's murder. Indeed, the song they sang, as they leaped about the cauldron, and threw in their infernal mixtures, was so similar to that of those "secret, black, and midnight hags," when they were going to "do the deed without a name," that I think the chorus in which they all joined, must have been gathered from some copy of the bedlam's accursed incantations. They repeated something very like the following stanzas, only more horrible:

1st Demon.

> *Round about the cauldron go.*
> *In the poisoned entrails, throw*
> *Drugs that in the coldest veins,*
> *Shoot incessant fiery pains,*
> *Herbs, that brought from hell's black door,*
> *Do its business slow and sure.*

All in Chorus.

> *Double, double, toil and trouble,*
> *Fire burn, and cauldron bubble.*

Several Demons successively, 1st, 2d, 3d, &c.

> *This shall scorch and sear the brain,*
> *This shall mad the heart with pain,*
> *This shall bloat the flesh with fire,*
> *This eternal thirst inspire,*
> *This shall savage lust inflame,*
> *This shall steel the soul to shame,*
> *This make all mankind contend*
> *'Tis their generous social friend.*

All in Chorus.

> *Double, double, toil and trouble',*

2d Demon.

> *This shall brutalize the mind,*
> *And to the corporal frame shall bind*
> *Fell disease of every kind,*
> *Dropsies, agues, fierce catarrhs,*
> *Pestilential inward wars,*
> *Fevers, gouts, convulsive starts,*
> *Racking spasms in vital parts.*
> *And men shall call the liquor good.*
> *The more with death it thicks the blood.*

All in Chorus.

> *Double, double, toil and trouble,*
> *Fire burn, and cauldron bubble.*

All the Demons in Full Chorus.

> *Mortals! yours the damning sin;*
> *Drink the maddening mixture in.*
> *It shall beat with fierce control,*
> *All the pulses of the soul.*
> *Sweet the poison, love it well,*
> *As the common path to hell.*
> *Let the charm of powerful trouble,*
> *Like a hell-broth boil and bubble.*
> *Double, double, toil and trouble,*
> *Fire burn, and cauldron bubble.*

They sang these devilish curses with dreadfully malignant satisfaction: and when all the processes in the preparation of the liquor were finished, with equal delight they proceeded to draft it in immense quantities into hogsheads and casks of every dimension. Into every vessel, as they filled it, they put a certain quantity of potash, lime, salts, and sulphuric acid, and then drove in the bung, and wrote upon the cask head, according as it suited their fancy. Some of the inscriptions were as follows:

"BEST LONDON PORTER, FROM DEACON JONES'S BREWERY."

"PALE ALE, OF THE PUREST MATERIALS."

"TEMPERANCE BEER, FROM DEACON JONES'S BREWERY"

"MILD AMERICAN PORTER, FOR FAMILY USE."

"BEST ALBANY ALE, FROM DEACON JONES'S BREWERY."

They also filled an immense multitude of bottles, from the fermenting tun, and packed them very neatly in strong square baskets, which they labelled in shining letters in these words:

"RESTORATIVE FOR WEAK CONSTITUTIONS—DEACON JONES'S BEST BOTTLED PORTER."

A very queer label, as I thought, was used by some, and that was:

"PALE ALE FOR THE NURSERY."

This work was finished just as it grew towards dawn, and having converted the Deacon's old distillery into an extensive brewery, they all vanished from the building; before light, in the same unaccountable manner in which they came into it.

In the morning, the Deacon walked out towards the establishment, not a little disturbed in his thoughts, as to what might have been going on ovenight. He found the outside of his distillery not very much altered, though a number of new windows were observable, surmounted with an out-jutting piece of plank like a penthouse, and covered with coarse blinds, through which the steam from the brewery was pouring in volumes. He thought likewise that the brick walls looked larger and longer than ever before, and more saturated with alcoholic perspiration, as though, indeed, they might have taken a midnight sweat. He found the man in blue and velvet walking about in the clear morning air, and surveying the scene apparently with peculiar satisfaction.

Without saving a word, the man took the Deacon by the arm, and led him into the building, and after pointing out all the extensive transformations and additions which had been accomplished during the night's work, he threw open the doors of an immense store-room, where the workmen had filled the casks of liquor for the Deacon, after the midnight brewing. "Now, Deacon," said the man, with a singularly expressive grin, "I think I have removed all your perplexities, and you may pursue your business on temperance grounds. Meantime we will be just as good friends as ever; for I do assure you that so long as you manage this brewery as I have begun it. you will, be doing my work quite as effectually as you were while you were carrying on the distillery." With that he politely lifted his three-cornered hat, passed gravely out of the building, and the Deacon saw him no more.

The Deacon was greatly puzzled. He knew not what to think of his strange companion, and for a time he hardly knew whether to be glad or sorry for the acquisition of wealth which he saw before him. Especially was he perplexed by the language of the man, when he said, "You will be doing my work" He could not tell what to make of it, and it troubled him not a little. However, he soon became absorbed in the study of the new machinery, and began to be particularly pleased with the prodigious size of the tun for fermentation, and the vastness of the well-filled store-room. He thought he could almost swim a revenue cutter in the one, and pile more than a thousand hogsheads in the other.

In the couse of the day he got busily engaged in his brewery, and the liquor was sent into all parts of the country; and wherever it came, and whoever tasted it, it was pronounced the most delicious of all intoxicating liquors. Confirmed drunkards smacked their lips, and declared that if they could only live upon such liquor as that, they never would touch another drop of New England Rum in the world. The Deacon was very much pleased, and some time afterwards he was heard to say in the midst of a company of bloated beer-drinkers, that Mr. E. C. Delavan, of Albany, would do more to injure the temperance reformation, by his ill-judged crusades against wine and beer, than he had ever done to forward it by all his energetic efforts against rum and brandy. The besotted crew, one and all, applauded the speech of the Deacon, declaring that he had expressed their opinion precisely; for they had long thought that the temperance cause was greatly suffering from the imprudence and misguided zeal of its professed friends.

The Deacon continues his brewery on so great a scale, that even his devil-built fermentation tun is hardly large enough to supply the demands of his customers. It is said that he manufactures the best "Copenhagen Porter in the country:" but every time I see his advertisement, "Inquire at Deacon Jones's Brewery," I hear again the midnight curse of the demons, and think of the dreadful meaning of their leader's language to the Deacon, "You will, be doing my work."

Autobiography Of

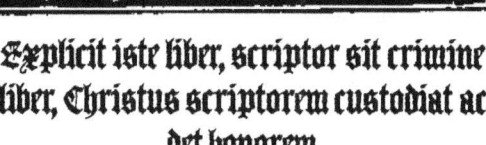

Explicit iste liber, scriptor sit crimine liber, Christus scriptorem custodiat ac det honorem

Ὥσπερ ξένοι χαίρουσιν ἰδεῖν πατρίδα, οὕτως καὶ οἱ γράφοντες ἰδεῖν βιβλίου τέλος

श्रीकृष्णार्पणमस्तु

書成矣，感盡天地

סלוע ארוב לאל חבש סלשנו סת

"of making many books there is no end; and much study is a weariness of the flesh"
- Ecclesiastes 12:12

BULKINGTON BOOKS